SPICING UP YOUR SPEAKING

DO YOU NEED A SPEAKER?

SPICING UP YOUR SPEAKING

247 Great Illustrations To Liven Up Your Talks

Simon Coupland

MONARCH
BOOKS

First published by Monarch Books in 2000.

ISBN 1 85424 471 X

British Library Cataloguing Data
A catalogue record for this book is available from the British Library.

Designed and produced for the publisher by
Gazelle Creative Productions,
Concorde House, Grenville Place, Mill Hill, London NW7 3SA.

CONTENTS

ACKNOWLEDGEMENTS

As at the Oscars, there are a number of people whom I'd like to thank for making this book possible.

First, many thanks to those friends who've given me stories: Marit Mundahl Haslestad, Steve Wallace, Esther Bailey and Robin Marsland.

Thanks, too, to those publishers, organisations and individuals who have kindly given me permission to reproduce their material, too many to list here, but all acknowledged at the appropriate place. I have done all I can to track down the sources, but if I have failed to acknowledge a story correctly, I apologise – please contact the publishers to put me right. As in my previous book, I have acknowledged the place where I heard or read a particular story, although I am aware that in some instances it may have originated somewhere else.

Thanks to Tony Collins at Monarch for asking me to write this second book.

Especial thanks to J. John for all his inspiration and encouragement to 'chill out', and also for agreeing to write the Foreword.

Much love and thanks to Heather and Philippa for letting me disappear off into the study to work on the computer instead of spending time with them. At least it's finished now!

And last but by no means least, thanks to my dad, who first asked me to give a sermon all those years ago. It made page 3 of the *Evening Standard*: 'Simon, 17, Steps into Father's Pulpit' – though when I saw the other stories on the page it rather knocked the shine off! To him and to my mum this book is dedicated, with my love and thanks.

FOREWORD

Knowing the desperation of speakers around the world I reckon Simon could have charged at least double the price you paid!

Simon is showing as much generosity as any other preacher I have known – he is giving away all his material. The measure of the man is that he is willing to share with all of us the best of what he has collected and heard over the years. Many others would have kept it all to themselves.

But the very fact that this book is published is an illustration, a sign, an example that it's not about any of us anyway – it's about the kingdom of God. It's not about who we are, but who he is; it's not about what we've got, but what we've been given. Augustine said that the gospel was summed up in the Pauline phrase 'What have we got that we have not received... ' – it's all a gift. The very fact that Simon has compiled this for us is an example of that. Nothing belongs to any of us – it's all God's, to be used not for ourselves, but his kingdom. So there's an illustration the book provides us with before we even get to the content!

Many of us know the importance of reinforcing our points by down-to-earth, and if possible, humorous flavouring. We've read all the statistics about our listeners' concentration time, how making a point and illustrating it means our hearers are more likely to remember it. Of spicing up our talks, or adding salt and pepper to what could otherwise be a bland rather tasteless meal. If that's what you need then you'll find help here.

But that's not all. Look at Jesus. So many times his stories and parables, the pictures he painted for his followers and listeners weren't simply to illustrate the point. They contained the point, they communicated it in a way that those around him could hear, understand and respond to. It's not about pepping up an otherwise dull message, it's not about just driving that point home again or illustrating that carefully constructed sentence telling the good news. It's about the message. It's about the good news itself. Not just illustrating and flavouring, but making the point, spelling it out loud and clear – not to make us sound more interesting but to make the good news of Jesus accessible.

This is what Simon inspires us to do. This isn't a book of shortcuts or solutions. It's a book which demands more work of us in communicating the message of Jesus, challenging us to relate the message of the kingdom in the very things we see around us, in what we experience, in things we hear. One of this century's greatest theologians, Karl Barth, talked about the need for the church to tell *secular* parables of the kingdom, not as mere bait to get people interested in the gospel but as a way of actually telling the gospel itself.

While I have no doubt that everyone who picks up this book will find their speaking ministry enriched, I hope and pray that we don't just let Simon do our work for us. Rather, that we let the way he is so willing to *give* what he could have kept to himself, the way he wants everything to be for Jesus' glory, the way he is endeavouring to talk about the kingdom in ways people can understand – inspire us not only to deeper understanding but renewed commitment to communicate to this world: God's lost world.

J. John

FATHER, SON AND HOLY SPIRIT

1. FATHER (Athletics, Child of God, Encouragement, Endurance, Failure, God, Love, Perseverance, Race, Sons, Sport, Victory)

Derek Redmon achieved every athlete's dream by running in the British team at the Barcelona Olympics in 1992. But half way through his race he fell to the ground as a torn ligament left him writhing in pain. The other runners raced past, his hopes and dreams of Olympic gold lying in tatters on the track beside him.

But then, amazingly, as the television cameras rolled and the crowd cheered, he picked himself up and tried to run on. His legs buckled, and he had to slow to a walk, but still he kept going.

Then the spectators saw a man come onto the track. Security guards tried to stop him, but he was as determined as the runner. He put his arm around Derek's shoulder and encouraged him to keep going and finish the race. The crowd roared its approval as the two of them crossed the finishing line.

The man was Derek's father.

Source: Adapted from Phil Callaway, Daddy, I Blew Up the Shed (Harvest House, 1994), p 129.

Bible references: 1 Chronicles 17:13; Psalms 40; 73:1–2; 89:1; Isaiah 40:28–31; 41:10; Matthew 10:28–31; Luke 12:6–7; John 1:12–13;

14:23; Acts 20:24; 1 Corinthians 9:24–27; 2 Corinthians 12:9; Philippians 3:12–14; 4:13; Colossians 1:11; 2 Timothy 4:7–8; Hebrews 12:1–3; 1 John 3:1.

2. FATHER (Church, Forgiveness, Grace, Jesus, Love, Misinterpretation, Parables, Prodigal)

We all know the parable of the prodigal son. But the way in which many Christians have really seen Jesus and the Father is like this:

> There was a man who had two sons. The younger son said to his father, 'Father, give me my share of the estate.' So he divided his property between them. And the younger son went off to a distant country and there squandered his wealth in wild living. But when his money ran out and he was reduced to feeding pigs, he came to his senses and set off back home.
>
> But while he was still a long way off, his older brother came out to meet him. 'Look,' he said, 'the old man is still really angry with you. But I tell you what. He loves me, because while you've been off living it up, I've led a blameless life here and never done anything wrong. So I'll have a word with him for you and see if I can't get him to let you back in. You'll have to be good, though, and watch your step, because I warn you, one false move and you're out.'

And so we miss out on grace, go on trying hard to live a good life, and live in constant fear of the Father. We forget that in Jesus' version of the parable, it is he who ran to his son, threw his arms around him and kissed him, saying, 'Let's have a feast and celebrate!'

Source: Adapted from Tom Smail, The Forgotten Father (Hodder and Stoughton, 1987), p 139. Copyright © 1995 by Philip Yancey. Used by permission of Zondervan Publishing House.

Bible references: Luke 15; John 3:16–17; Romans 3:25–26; 2 Corinthians 5:18–19; 1 John 4:10.

3. JESUS (Advertising, Cheese, Marketing, Names, Humour)

An Israeli kibbutz that manufactured dairy products wanted to come up with a new name to improve their image and boost their sales. So they asked an American marketing company to suggest a catchy new brand name. The result? Cheeses of Nazareth.

Source: Adapted from The Daily Telegraph, 21 November 1998.

Bible references: Matthew 1:21.

4. CHRISTMAS (Christ, Humility, Incarnation, Jesus, Kenosis, Sin, the World, Humour)

It was the Christmas family service, and all the children were gathered around the crib at the front of the church. 'Look in the crib,' said the curate, 'and see if you can tell me what's missing.'

The children peered into the crib. Everything seemed to be there. 'Are all the people there?' he asked. They checked carefully: Mary, Joseph, baby Jesus, wise men, shepherds, an angel; yes, they were all there. 'And is everything in the stable?' he asked. They looked again: a donkey, a cow, straw, a manger; yes, everything was there. 'But what's missing?' the curate asked again. They shook their heads. They couldn't think of anything.

'This is what's missing!' he said, and emptied a bucket of manure onto the church floor.

Source: Simon Coupland.

Bible references: Matthew 20:28; Mark 10:45; Luke 2:1–16; John 1:1–14; 13:3–12; 2 Corinthians 8:9; Philippians 2:5–11; Hebrews 2:11–17; 5:8.

5. INCARNATION (Christ, Christmas, Creation, Fear, Fish, God, Grace, Humility, Jesus, Kenosis, Love, Salvation, the World)

Philip Yancey writes:

> I learned about incarnation when I kept a salt-water aquarium. Management of a marine aquarium, I discovered, is no easy task. I had to run a portable chemical laboratory to monitor the nitrate levels and the ammonia content. I pumped in vitamins and antibiotics and sulpha drugs and enough enzymes to make a rock grow. I filtered the water through glass fibres and charcoal, and exposed it to ultraviolet light. You would think, in view of all the energy expended on their behalf, that my fish would at least be grateful. Not so. Every time my shadow loomed above the tank they dove for cover into the nearest shell. They showed one 'emotion' only: fear. Although I opened the lid and dropped in food on a regular schedule, three times a day, they responded to each visit as a sure sign of my designs to torture them. I could not convince them of my true concern.
>
> To my fish I was deity. I was too large for them, my actions too incomprehensible. My acts of mercy they saw as cruelty; my attempts at healing they

viewed as destruction. To change their perceptions, I began to see, would require a form of incarnation. I would have to become a fish and 'speak' to them in a language they could understand.

Source: Taken from Philip Yancey, The Jesus I Never Knew (Zondervan Publishing House, 1995), pp 38–39.

Bible references: Matthew 20:28; Mark 10:45; Luke 2:1–16; John 1:1–14; 13:3–12; 2 Corinthians 8:9; Philippians 2:5–11; Hebrews 2:11–17; 1 John 4:9–10.

6. INCARNATION (Christ, Christmas, Example, God, Grace, Humility, Jesus, Kenosis, Love, Royalty, Salvation, the World)

It's impossible to imagine going up to London to see Buckingham Palace, and finding the Queen standing outside at a bus stop, waiting for a bus. But that is precisely what the people of Oslo saw during the oil crisis of 1973: the then king, Olav the Fifth, catching the tram up to the ski slopes like any other ordinary citizen. His bodyguard went with him, of course, but the king felt that if the rest of the population was being asked to leave their cars at home to save energy, he should set an example. So like everybody else, he boarded the tram outside the royal palace and, skis in hand, headed for the slopes outside the city.

Source: Simon Coupland.

Bible references: Matthew 1:18–25; 20:28; Mark 10:45; Luke 1–2; John 1:1–14; 13:3–12; 2 Corinthians 8:9; Philippians 2:5–11; Hebrews 2:11–17; 5:8; 1 John 4:9–10.

7. INCARNATION (Christ, Christmas, Creation, God, Grace, Humility, Insects, Jesus, Kenosis, Love, Salvation, Sin, Suffering, the World)

Billy Graham tells of the time when he and his son were out walking in the forest and they trod on an anthill. They could see the ants milling around in confusion: some were wounded, some were dead, others were carrying away the dead. Billy said to his son, 'Wouldn't it be marvellous if we could become ants and go down there and tell them that it was an accident, that we didn't do it on purpose.' Then he thought to himself how amazing it is that Jesus became a man, that the Son of God came down from the glory of heaven and became like one of us. And he didn't do it to say sorry for what God had done to us, but to rescue us from what we had done to each other.

Source: Billy Graham, Cambridge 1980.

Bible references: Matthew 1:18–25; 20:28; Mark 10:45; Luke 1–2; John 1:1–14; 13:3–12; 2 Corinthians 8:9; Philippians 2:5–11; Hebrews 2:11–17; 5:8; 1 John 4:9–10.

8. THE CROSS (Army, Atonement, Christ, Conditioning, Crucifixion, Human nature, Humiliation, Incarnation, Jesus, Kenosis, Military service, Nakedness, Ridicule, Salvation, Suffering)

Will Willimon, the American writer and preacher, tells how he was called up into the US Army when he was a student.

> The first thing they did on the first day was to put the new conscripts in a huge room, make them take all their clothes off, and then stand in line for three

hours. He said, 'It does something to you, 800 men standing in line for three hours, with nothing to protect you but the information sheet that you're holding. And then at the end of the line came the most dreaded thing they could do to you when you're nineteen or twenty in the late 1960s – they shaved your hair. And it seemed so pointless. Why would the US Army feel the need to do that?'

Then a sergeant explained what was going on. He said, 'Look, I know when you were in Officer Training Corps they said the Army was training you to be leaders, training you to use your gifts of leadership.' He said, 'That's crap. You're being trained to kill people. All right? And because you're all in college it's going to take us about five weeks to make a soldier out of you. You're all some kind of individualists who think you know what's best. And we're going to teach you to obey orders and to move as one and to not ask questions and to go in and to go against everything you've been taught for your whole life. And the beginning of it is shaving your head.'

Will Willimon says, 'I realised the Army knew exactly what it was doing. In order to give somebody a new existence, even a corrupted and sad one like that, you start out by stripping them naked, get all that stuff off them by which they distinguish themselves and make themselves look like somebody. You strip them down to nothing, and in about twenty-four hours you can do anything with them you want to.

'It was on the cross that Jesus commended his spirit to God. But of course when you've been stripped and picked clean, and held up to the ridicule of the world, there's really nowhere else to go but God. The ultimate humiliation. And yet Paul says, that is the way that leads to life.'

Source: Will Willimon, International Congress of Preachers, London 1997.

Bible references: Psalm 22; Isaiah 53:2–3; Matthew 16:24–25; 20:19; 26:2; 27:32–50; Mark 8:34–35; 15:21–37; Luke 9:23–24; 24:26–46; John 19:16–37; Romans 5:8; 1 Corinthians 1:18–24; 2 Corinthians 5:14,21; 13:4; Galatians 3:13; Philippians 2:5–11; Hebrews 5:7–10; 12:2; 1 Peter 2:24.

9. ATONEMENT (Christ, Cross, Holocaust, Jesus, Jews, Love, Nazism, Sacrifice, Salvation, Second World War)

In 1944 the Jews in Nazi Germany were being exterminated. And in the rest of occupied Europe they were being hunted down, rounded up, herded onto trains and shipped off to concentration camps. But in the Hungarian capital, Budapest, one man, a thirty-two-year-old Swedish businessman named Raoul Wallenberg, decided that something must be done to stop this terrible crime. And he realised that he was one of the few people who could do something to stop it. That October, as hundreds of Jews were being forced onto a train bound for the death camp at Auschwitz, Wallenberg appeared on the platform, handing out documents which said that these people were Swedish citizens and could not therefore be deported. In the course of the next three months, Wallenberg gave these special passes to thousands of men, women and children – all of them Jews. Without those documents, they were as good as dead. With them, they could live.

In the new year, even though the fighting was drawing closer, Wallenberg chose to stay in Hungary to carry on with his life-saving work. When the Red Army reached Budapest in January 1945, he went to see the Russian commander. He was never seen again. The Soviet authorities later admitted that he had died in a prison camp. He gave his life so that tens of thousands of others might live.

Source: Simon Coupland.

Bible references: Isaiah 53:4–7; Matthew 20:28; 26:26–28; Mark 10:45; 14:22–24; Luke 22:19–20; John 3:14–17; Romans 4:25; 5:6–11; 8:1–4; 1 Corinthians 5:7; 15:3; 2 Corinthians 5:14–15; 1 Thessalonians 5:10; 1 Timothy 2:5–6; Titus 2:14; Hebrews 9:15,28; 1 Peter 1:18–19; 2:24–25; 3:18.

10. AMAZING DISCOVERIES (Christ, Cross, Crown of thorns, Crucifixion, Jesus, Media, Newspapers, Tabloids, Turin shroud, Humour)

The American tabloid the *Weekly World News* likes to make sure its scoops are really sensational. As well as reporting the discovery of the bones of Adam and Eve – and their baby daughter (see story 207) – they also claimed in their issue of 21 September 1993 that the cross on which Jesus was crucified had been found in the Holy Land. According to the story, a 'leading archaeologist' named Dr Ronald Worthin (strangely unknown to other biblical archaeologists!) had found not only the true cross but also the crown of thorns with which the soldiers had mocked Jesus. The paper proudly reported the 'proof' that these remarkable discoveries really were the genuine articles. According to Dr Worthin, DNA tests had been carried out on the bloodstains found on the cross, which matched the blood found on the Shroud of Turin, thus proving that both sets of blood came from the same man! (Not surprisingly, the paper failed to mention the fact that radio carbon dating puts the origin of the shroud some time in the middle ages.)

Source: Adapted from Biblical Archaeology Review, January/February 1997.

Bible references: Matthew 27:29,31–35; Mark 15:17,20–24; Luke 23:26,33; John 19:2–5,16–18.

11. PRAYER (Christ, Death, Desert, Faith, Feelings, Jesus, Old age, Peace, Presence of God, Sickness, Silence, Simplicity, Wilderness)

An elderly Scotsman was on his deathbed. He wasn't afraid of dying or of death, but he was having trouble praying. When his pastor visited him one day the old man told him about his problem. 'It just doesn't seem real to me,' he said.

'Why don't you put a chair next to your bed,' the minister suggested, 'and imagine that Jesus is sitting in it. Then talk to him the same way that you're talking to me.'

A few days later the pastor received a phone call from the man's daughter, who'd been nursing her father. 'Pastor,' she said, 'I wanted you to know that my father died this afternoon. I'd just finished getting his lunch and I went to check on him, and he was gone. He looked just the same as when I'd left him, except for one odd little thing. His hand was resting on the chair beside the bed.'

Source: Adapted from Steve Brown, Approaching God: How to Pray (Summit Publishing Ltd, 1996), p 62.

Bible references: Deuteronomy 31:6–8; 1 Kings 8:57; Psalms 23:4; 46; 91; 121; Isaiah 41:10,13–14; 43:1–5; Matthew 28:20; Luke 2:28–32.

12. THE HOLY SPIRIT (Belief, Children, the Creed, God, the Trinity)

Most people can imagine God the Father, the creator, and most of us can picture God the Son, Jesus as a human being. But lots of people have difficulty imagining the Holy Spirit. Professor Gordon Fee, who lectures about the New Testament at a theological college, tells of a student who once said, 'God the Father makes perfectly good sense to me, and God the Son I can quite understand, but the Holy Spirit is a grey, oblong blur.' He's not alone in that!

Fee goes on to tell the story of a friend of his who was giving a children's talk at Pentecost. She was trying to get across the fact that the Spirit of God is real, even though you can't see him. Like many a preacher before and after her, she tried to illustrate the point by blowing a piece of paper off her hand. The Spirit is like that, she said: you can see the paper moving, even though the wind is invisible. At which point a six-year-old boy blurted out, 'But I want the wind to be un-invisible!' There are lots of adults who feel the same way.

Professor Fee concludes: 'So the practising creed for many Christians becomes: "I believe in God the Father, I believe in Jesus Christ, God's Son, but I wonder about the Holy Ghost."'

Source: Adapted from Gordon Fee, Paul, the Spirit and the People of God (Hendrickson, 1996), p 24, 37.

Bible references: Ezekiel 37:9–14; John 3:8; 14:8–9; 20:24–29; Acts 2:2; 4:31; 1 Corinthians 2:9–14; 1 Peter 1:8.

13. GOD (Advertising, Computers, Gambling, Lottery, Modern life, Money, Prize draw, Raffle, Wealth, Humour)

The Assemblies of God church in Bushnell in Florida, was surprised to receive a letter addressed to God from the American Family Publishers. 'God, we've been searching for you!' it began, promisingly enough. It then went on to explain that he had been lucky enough to be assigned one of the potential winning numbers in their multi-million dollar sweepstakes draw.

'What an incredible fortune there would be for God!' it went on. 'Could you imagine the looks you'd get from your neighbours? But don't just sit there, God,' it continued, reminding him that he had to attach his colour-coded seal to the official reply form and send it in before the deadline to make sure that he had a chance of winning the top prize.

Source: Adapted from The Daily Telegraph, 22 March 1997.

14. ATTRIBUTES OF GOD (Grace, Heresy, History, Human nature, Jesus, Mary, Sects, Humour)

In 1854 the British government sent a boat up the Yangtze river to Nanking to find out about a rebel Chinese movement based there which claimed to be Christian. The Chinese then sent the commander of the ship, whose name was Captain Mellersh, a list of fifty questions which they wanted him to answer. Here is how the list begins:

'The questions I have to ask are these –
You nations having worshipped God for so long a time, does any one among you know,

1. How tall God is, or how broad?
2. What his appearance or colour is?
3. How large his abdomen is?
4. What kind of beard he grows?
5. What colour his beard is?
6. How long his beard is?
7. What cap he wears?
8. What kind of clothes he wears?
9. Whether his first wife was the same Heavenly Mother as brought forth the Heavenly Elder Brother Jesus?
10. Whether he has had any other son born to him since the birth of Jesus?
11. Whether he has had just one son, or whether, like us mortals, a great many?
12. Whether he is able to write poetry?
13. How rapidly can he write poetry?
14. How fierce his disposition is?
15. How great his generosity is?

Source: Quoted in Jonathan Spence, God's Chinese Son (Harper Collins, 1996), pp 230–231 (see also A Dose of Salts, story 246).

Bible references: Exodus 15:11–13; 34:6–7; Numbers 14:18–19; 1 Kings 8:23–24; Nehemiah 9:17–19; Psalms 35:10; 86; 89; 103; 113:5–9; Isaiah 40:18–28; 46:5–6; Jeremiah 10:6–16; 51:15–19; John 14:8–9; Colossians 1:15.

GOD AT WORK

15. ANSWERED PRAYER (Forgiveness, Hope, Intercession, Media, Newspapers, Peace, Politics, Reconciliation, South Africa)

The journalists on *The Guardian* are not known for their religious faith. Yet on the day after Nelson Mandela was sworn in as President of the new, multi-racial South Africa, correspondent Rian Malan wrote:

> It is time to talk of many things, of bullets unfired and hatchets buried, of discarded flak jackets and peace in the land. Five months, even five weeks ago, I was certain that our first free elections would be a bloodbath. I was wrong. These are small and snide times, and I am a cynic, but still, it must be said, I do believe prayers were realised, and that what has happened in this country in the past ten days cannot really be accounted for in terms of rational analysis. Least of all mine.

Source: The Guardian, 11 May 1994, Reproduced with kind permission, The Guardian ©.

Bible references: Genesis 18:23–32; Isaiah 62:6–7; Matthew 6:9–10; Luke 11:1–2; 18:1–7; Romans 12:12; 2 Corinthians 1:10–11; Ephesians 6:18; Philippians 1:19; Colossians 4:2; 1 Thessalonians 5:17; 1 Timothy 2:1–4; James 5:16–18.

16. CONVERSION (Alpha, Books, Conviction, Forgiveness, Holy Spirit, Joy, Sin, Testimony, Witness)

Andy Green was a technical services manager in an insurance company, in his own words a 'confirmed atheist'. A Christian colleague gave him a copy of the evangelistic booklet *Why Jesus?* and the Alpha course book, *Questions of Life*. Andy put them in his briefcase and left them there for a couple of weeks. I'll let him tell the story:

> One night, when my wife was out and the kids were in bed, I decided that as there was nothing on television and I didn't want to listen to any music, I would read the booklet.
>
> Page by page things started to ring true – subjects like, 'Something missing in one's life'. Nothing dramatic happened until I got to the second to last page – the prayer for forgiveness. I read the first five words, 'Lord Jesus, I am sorry... ' and I broke down into floods of tears. I couldn't read the rest of it. I just kept saying, 'I am so sorry, I am so sorry.'
>
> I didn't think I had been so bad. I could be sarcastic. I could be critical. I could be judgmental and I was. But all of a sudden I thought, 'No, it doesn't matter whether it is robbery, murder, rape, telling a lie, being judgmental or sarcastic – to God these are all sins. They're all wrong.'
>
> All of a sudden I started to feel this pulling. It was as if everything I had ever done wrong was being pulled and all of a sudden I was filled with the most incredible sense of joy. I had never experienced anything like it before. I finished the leaflet, picked up *Questions of Life* and ran downstairs. I read to about

two thirds of the way through when my wife came in.

The booklet says that after praying the prayer you ought to tell someone, so I thought, 'I'll tell Sally.' She looked at me as if I had gone mad.

I got up the next morning, drove off smiling like a Cheshire cat, and arrived at work. Work is quite pressured, in fact extremely pressured. I have a team of fifteen people and four senior people who represent various areas of the team for me. Two of them looked at me and asked if I was all right. I said, 'Fine.' They said, 'OK. Nothing's up then?' Off they went.

A couple of hours later they came back in again. 'Are you sure there's nothing wrong?'

'No, fine. Does it look like something's the matter?'

'No, but it looks like something's going on.'

I said, 'I think something's gone on, actually.' Off they went.

The next day they came back in. They were a bit more forceful. 'Now look, what's going on? Are you going to tell us?' Eventually, a couple of hours later, they came back in and put a couple of chairs across my doorway. They said, 'We are staging a sit-in. We must know what's going on.'

These two are not Christians. They said, 'Are you on something?' I said, 'No.'

They said, 'Well, what is it then? Can we have some?'

I said, 'In actual fact, yes, you can.'

'What is it, then?'

I said, 'Do you really want to know?'

They said, 'Yes!'

'Be prepared for a shock,' I said. 'I've become a Christian.'

They almost fell off their chairs. One of them looked at me, straight in the eyes, and you could see absolute disbelief in his face. After a long silence, he looked at me and said, 'I am really pleased for you.' The other one was still pinching himself.

Source: UK Focus, October 1998. Reproduced by kind permission of Holy Trinity, Brompton.

Bible references: Matthew 5:18–19; Romans 1:16; 2 Corinthians 5:17–20; Ephesians 1:19–20; 2:1–5; Colossians 4:5–6; James 2:10–11; 1 Peter 3:15–16.

17. CONVERSION (Acceptance, Addiction, Church, Drugs, Freedom, Healing, Holy Spirit, Hospitality, Liberation, Love, Peace, Restoration, Salvation, Self-esteem, Slavery, Testimony)

Bob Light was addicted to heroin for twenty-seven years. During that time, he says:

> The needle had become the main focus in my life. Every two hours, I needed to put a needle in my arm for a release. Heroin took me to mental hospitals, rehab centres and even a padded cell in prison. My life was a living hell. I hated myself. I seemed to destroy everybody and everything I touched. I didn't care if I died and there were many times when I was nearly successful; it seemed the only way out. I didn't believe it was possible to live without taking drugs.

And then, by chance, he met a man who offered him a place to stay, an evangelist, who told him about Jesus. Bob goes on:

Even though I was still injecting I went to church on Sundays and was amazed at the love I was shown by Christians. They made me feel part of their family and accepted me. During this time Jesus started to show me that I wasn't worthless, but chosen and special. The revelation that Christ had chosen me was the start of my self-acceptance and healing.

I asked God to help me, and he did. I still have to pinch myself some days when I realise just how simple it was. No cold turkey, no agony, no sweats. Just freedom from twenty-seven years of slavery to addiction. With Jesus, I was given a brand-new start. Within twenty days he set me free from all my addictions: I went through no withdrawals. My mind, which was confused and totally messed up, has been healed and is being renewed daily. I now have peace in my mind and life.

I have now been freed from drugs for five years with not one relapse. Jesus has been restoring everything to me that I lost and more.

Source: Adapted from Renewal, November 1998.

Bible references: Deuteronomy 7:6–8; 32:9–14; Psalm 107; Isaiah 43:1–4; 61:1; Luke 4:18; John 8:31–36; Romans 5:1–2; 6:16–23; 7:24–25; 8:1–2; 2 Corinthians 3:17; 5:17–20; Ephesians 1:19–20; 2:1–5; 1 Peter 2:9–10.

18. DELIVERANCE (The Bible, Demons, the Devil, Evil, Exorcism, Jesus, Medicine, Miracles, New Testament, Possession, Prayer, Psychiatry, Science, Spirits, Spiritual warfare)

David Instone Brewer studied psychiatry as part of his medical training. As a Christian, he knew the stories of Jesus' exorcisms, but he thought that psychiatry offered a much better explanation for them than what he regarded as the old-fashioned, fundamentalist Bible teaching he'd been brought up on. Then one day when he was sitting by a patient's bed, waiting for him to wake up, he started to pray for the man, silently. At that moment the patient sat up and said in a loud voice, quite unlike his usual voice, 'Leave him alone: he belongs to us.'

David wasn't sure what to do next, so he didn't say anything. He knew that he shouldn't mention demons or demon possession, because that might feed the delusions of someone who was mentally ill, so he just carried on praying silently. He thought he remembered that Jesus rebuked evil spirits, so he tried that, again without saying anything out loud, but it just triggered another angry outburst. Now he knew he was out of his depth, so he just kept praying silently, and after a while the man screamed and fell back on the bed. A little later he woke up, with no memory at all of what had happened. What was more, he said that the voices in his head which had made him depressed and even suicidal had gone.

Over the coming weeks David continued to pray for the man, always silently, and nearly always when the man was asleep or under hypnosis. The amazing thing was that the spirits in the man – because by now he was convinced that that was what he was dealing with – answered his unspoken questions. In silent prayer he would ask the demons their names, and they would answer out loud. Some gave Greek names like *thanatoi* (spirits of death), which made the man suicidal, or *phoboi* (spirits of fear), which made him anxious. Others were lying spirits: at first they claimed to be spirits of kindness or innocence, but when pressed they turned out to be the opposite. Each time, when David continued to pray, they left, and did not return. To his astonishment, he found himself imitating what Jesus had done in the Gospels, despite his scepticism of such a short time earlier.

Over time the man improved to such an extent that he was able to leave hospital, and in the end he was completely free of his former problems – cured as far as the psychiatrists were concerned, delivered as David now believed. And he remained so afterwards.

Source: Adapted from David Instone Brewer, 'Jesus and the Psychiatrists' in Anthony Lane, ed. The Unseen World (Paternoster, 1996), pp 140–143.

Bible references: Matthew 4:24; 8:16,28–34; 9:32–33; 10:1,8; 12:22–29; 15:21–28; 17:14–18; Mark 1:23–27,32–34,39; 3:11–15, 22–27; 5:1–20; 6:7; 7:24–30; 9:17–27; 16:17; Luke 4:33–36,41; 8:26–39; 9:1; 10:17–20; 11:14–26; Acts 5:16; 8:7; 16:18; 19:13–16.

19. FAITH (Africa, Afterlife, Boldness, Confidence, Conversion, Death, Easter, Evangelism, Judgement, Opposition, Resurrection, Suffering, Witness)

One Easter Sunday morning a pastor in Uganda, Kefa Sempangi, was on his way home after taking the morning service when he was ambushed by a gang of armed men. 'We are going to kill you,' said the leader. 'If you have anything to say, say it before you die.'

Kefa was terrified. He thought to himself, 'They won't need to kill me, I'm going to drop dead anyway.' But then, he said, 'From far away I heard a voice, and I was astonished to realise that it was my own. "I do not need to plead my own cause," I heard myself saying. "I am a dead man already. My life is dead and hidden in Christ. It is your lives that are in danger, you are dead in your sins. I will pray to God that after you have killed me, he will spare you from eternal destruction."'

That came as quite a surprise to Kefa, but what happened next was even more amazing. The leader of the gang, who a moment earlier had been threatening to kill him, visibly changed. He said to the pastor, 'Will you pray for us now?' And suddenly the tables were turned. Instead of Kefa facing death, he was able to offer these men life – eternal life. And so he prayed with them, there and then. All five men in that gang went on to become members of Kefa's church.

Source: Adapted from Richard Bewes, The Resurrection – Fact or Fiction? (Lion, 1989), p 47.

Bible references: Matthew 10:19–20; Mark 13:11; Luke 12:11–12; 21:13–15; John 10:28–29; Romans 6:2–11; Galatians 2:20; Ephesians 2:1–6; 6:19–20; Colossians 2:13; 3:3; 2 Timothy 4:17–18; Hebrews 11:13–16.

20. POWER OF GOD (Africa, Answered Prayer, Boldness, Confidence, Evangelism, Evil, Faith, God, Miracles, Mission, Missionaries, Opposition, Other faiths, Prayer, Signs, Tribal religion, Witness)

Henry was a missionary who worked in remote areas of Africa in the 1920s and 1930s. He used his skills as a linguist to teach the natives to read, and in every village he started by building a school hut, with bamboo walls and a thatched roof. But everywhere he had to put up with the hostility of local witch doctors, who saw what Henry was doing as undermining their role and threatening their religion.

On one occasion, the local witch doctor told Henry that if he didn't leave the village, the tribe's god would burn the school to the ground. Henry wasn't afraid of tribal gods, but he was afraid that the witch doctor might try to set fire to his hut. So it came as a shock when in the early hours of the morning, there was an almighty storm, and lightning hit the school and burned it to the ground.

Early the next morning the witch doctor appeared with his followers and told Henry to leave. But Henry, in a sudden outburst of God-given boldness, said that his God, the God of the Bible, was more powerful than the tribe's god. That very night, Henry said, the village totem pole would be struck by lightning and destroyed.

As soon as the witch doctor had gone, Henry began to wonder what on earth he had done. Everyone in the village had heard what he'd said. There was no going back; all he could do was pray. And pray he did. Early the following morning, there was a great flash of lightning and the village totem pole was burned to the ground. Henry stayed. The school was rebuilt. The people learned to read. And believed in Henry's God.

Source: Adapted from Calvin Miller, A Hunger for Meaning (InterVarsity Press, 1984), pp 108–109.

Bible references: Genesis 15:7–17; 1 Kings 18:20–40; 2 Kings 1:1–17; 2 Chronicles 14:11; 32:1–22; Acts 4:23–31.

21. REPENTANCE (Answered prayer, Atheism, Christianity, Commandments, Communism, Faith, God, Intercession, KGB, Miracles, Politics, Russia, Soviet Union)

In September 1991 a group of American evangelicals received an amazing letter from the Supreme Soviet in Moscow. They were invited to travel to the Soviet Union and meet its leaders, including President Gorbachev, to tell them what the Christian faith could do to help their nation. The openness they encountered in Russia amazed them even more. For instance, in the headquarters of the KGB they met General Nikolai Stolyarov, one of the vice-chairmen of the secret police. He said to them,

> Political questions cannot be decided until there is sincere repentance, a return to faith by the people. That is the cross I must bear. I have been a member of the Party for twenty years. In our study of scientific atheism, we were taught that religion divides people. Now we see the opposite: love for God can only unite... The time has come to repent of the past. We have broken the ten commandments, and for this we pay today.

Source: Adapted from Philip Yancey, Praying with the KGB (Multnomah, 1992), p 33.

Bible references: Leviticus 26:40–42; 1 Samuel 7:6; 1 Kings 8:46–49; 2 Chronicles 6:36–39; 7:14; Nehemiah 1:5–7; 9:1–3; Psalms 32; 51; Isaiah 59:12–13; Daniel 9:4–6; 1 Timothy 2:1–4; James 5:16; 1 John 1:8–10.

22. RESTING IN THE SPIRIT (Forgiveness, Healing, Holy Spirit, Prayer, Tongues)

The Roman Catholic speaker and writer Francis MacNutt tells how, at a healing meeting, he prayed for a fellow priest, Benedict Haren. Although he only prayed briefly in tongues, Father Haren was overcome by the Holy Spirit and sank to the floor, where he lay for over two hours. Afterwards he said that during that time God had taken him through his entire life, stage by stage, explaining the significance of various painful episodes in his past, and healing their wounds. He was reminded of incidents which he had almost forgotten, but which had actually left him with deep scars. As he put it in his own words,

> During the time I 'rested in the Spirit' I not only realised that I had not forgiven certain people, a fact I was unaware of before, but I also learned more about the nature and demands of Christian forgiveness while lying on the ground there than I had ever understood from talks or books. The Holy Spirit gave me a much deeper insight on this subject, which I regard as one of the major spiritual blessings of my life.

Source: Adapted from Francis MacNutt, Overcome by the Spirit (Eagle, 1991), p 54.

Bible references: Jeremiah 23:9; Daniel 8:18; 10:8–9,17; Matthew 6:12–15; 18:21–35; Mark 11:25–26; Luke 6:37; John 20:23; Ephesians 4:32; Colossians 3:13; Revelation 1:17.

23. SELF-ESTEEM (Abortion, Cleansing, Conversion, Dreams, Forgiveness, Freedom, Guilt, Healing, Liberation, Love, Rejection, Salvation, Slavery, Testimony, Visions)

Wendy was trapped by rejection and guilt and fear. Her mother had died when she was only three, and her stepmother had always hated her. Wendy was coloured, and her stepmother would scrub her in scalding hot water until her skin was red and raw. 'You're ugly!' she would shout. 'You'll never have a boyfriend! No one could ever love you!' So Wendy grew up believing she was ugly, stupid and totally unworthy of anyone's love. And even though she did well at school, had boyfriends, and came top of her college course, when she got pregnant it just proved her stepmother's point. 'I always said she was useless!' she sneered. 'So much for her brains!'

Bringing up a child as a single parent was hard work, and when Wendy once again found that she was pregnant, she decided to have an abortion. Even though it seemed the only solution, she still grieved over the twins she knew she had been carrying. As time went by, things looked up. Wendy got a good job, and married a man who offered her a new start. Yet still those feelings of rejection and guilt clung to her, and some days she would take three or four baths to try and wash herself clean. And when she became pregnant she was terrified that God would take this child away to punish her for the abortion.

But then one night she had a dream. She saw Christ smiling down at her. He made her feel clean and beautiful, the way she longed to be, and she stretched out her arms towards him. But then she woke up. It was just a dream.

Not long after that Wendy started going to church, but she couldn't believe what the pastor said, that she could be forgiven. She thought that all she deserved was punishment and rejection. But as the minister prayed with her, and she asked Jesus to come into her life, she felt a tremendous sense of liberation from the past and cleansing. 'I felt white all the way through,' she said, 'and I even lost my fear of losing the baby.'

Only a few weeks later, it was through Wendy's prayers that the well-known writer Jennifer Rees Larcombe was healed – suddenly, immediately, totally and miraculously. And then Wendy knew for sure that 'in God's eyes no one is second class'.

Source: Adapted from Jennifer Rees Larcombe, Unexpected Healing (Hodder & Stoughton, 1991), pp 199–205.

Bible references: Deuteronomy 7:6–8; 32:9–14; Psalms 32:1–2; 51; Isaiah 43:1–4; Ezekiel 36:25–27; John 3:16–18; 8:31–36; Romans 7:24–25; 8:1–2; 1 Corinthians 6:11; 2 Corinthians 5:17–20; Galatians 3:13–14; Ephesians 1:19–20; 2:1–5; Hebrews 9:13–14; 1 Peter 2:9–10; 1 John 1:7–9.

24. A SIGN (Answered prayer, Army, Conversion, Creation, Faith, God, Presence of God, Radio, Salvation, Suffering, War)

Frank Collins was a soldier in the SAS. A hard man, from a hard family background. In the Army the general attitude was that religion is for wimps, but then Frank met Special Forces soldiers from the US for whom Christianity was at the heart of their life. One of them was a man named Larry, who became a good friend. Frank questioned, and argued, and again and again went back to the same three questions. How can you believe in a creator God, when everyone knows about evolution? How can you believe in a God of love, when there's so much suffering? And how can you reconcile being a soldier and being a Christian?

Then one night, on an exercise in a forest in Germany, he prayed.

> 'God, if you really exist and you really are out there listening to me, then please give me a sign of some kind. If you don't send me a sign tonight then that means once and for all that Larry is talking a load of nonsense.'
>
> I lie there waiting. Everything is still. Occasionally I open my eyes and glance around sneakily. Just in case an angel's standing there, glowing in the dark. But there's no angel. There's nothing. I go to sleep. See. It's all just a load of nonsense.

Dawn's about to break. I send our signals, then I tune the radio to the BBC World Service. The next programme is an interview with someone who was in Bomber Command in the war.

The interviewee turns out to be a metallurgist. He's going to be asked three questions, the interviewer explains. How can God have created the world in a few days when, as a scientist, he must agree that it evolved over aeons? How can he believe in God's love when he has seen so much suffering? And how can you be a soldier and a Christian, when Christians don't kill people and soldiers do?

I lie as if electrified. My three questions. This man is going to answer them.

I lie listening to him. He's saying nothing new, nothing I haven't heard before from Larry, but the rightness of what I hear almost pushes me out of bed. I am sure now that God has sent me a sign. This voice on the radio has been speaking to me.

For the first time in my life I have a sense of God. He is there, He is all around me. I recognise that my life will never be the same again.

Source:

Bible references: Genesis 15:7–17; Exodus 3:12; 4:1–9; Judges 6:17–22,36–40; 1 Kings 18:20–40; 2 Kings 20:8–11.

Note: Although Frank Collins later took his own life in tragic circumstances, there is no reason to doubt the genuineness of his conversion. Indeed, his death makes his remarkable story all the more poignant, and his agent felt that Frank would have been pleased to see this extract from Baptism of Fire reproduced here.

25. UNANSWERED PRAYER (Africa, Desert, Disappointment, Endurance, Evangelism, Failure, Frustration, God, Hardship, Intercession, Ministry, Mission, Missionaries, Patience, Perseverance, Sickness, Silence of God, Success, Suffering, Tribal religion, Wilderness, Witness)

Bob and Barbara were Canadian missionaries working in East Africa. For twelve years they worked hard witnessing to a particular tribe without making a single convert. But then at last the breakthrough came. The chief's son, whose name was Ochi, became a Christian, and they baptised him early one Sunday morning in the nearby river. That opened the gates, and a number of other villagers came to faith as well.

Everything seemed to be going well: the church was growing, Bob and Barbara were helping the young Christians to grow in their faith, but then disaster struck. Both missionaries were laid low by a mystery illness. Day after day they were so weak that all they could do was lie in bed and pray. And they did. They prayed for the converts, they prayed for protection for the church, and they prayed for their healing, but God did not answer their prayers.

As the months went by and their health failed to improve, the new converts started to drift back to their tribal religion, and in the end, broken in health and in spirit, Bob and Barbara went back to Canada. But though it may sound like it, the story doesn't end there.

Nearly twenty years later their son, Nick, went to Africa on a business trip, and visited the village where his parents had lived so many years before. To his amazement, he found that the church, which his parents had left struggling and on the point of collapse, was strong and vibrant. When he asked what had happened, the local people told him the story. The departure of his parents, far from being the nail in the coffin, had actually led to the church's rebirth, because the local Christians had realised that with the missionaries gone, it was up to them to share their faith with their fellow villagers. So they did. And instead of dying, the church grew in numbers and in strength.

Nick said, 'I'm sorry Dad never lived to see his prayers answered. He went to his grave a disappointed man.'

Source: Adapted from Michael Apichella in Renewal, June 1994.

Bible references: Genesis 45:4–8; 50:20; Proverbs 16:9; 21:31; Isaiah 46:10; 55:9–11; Jeremiah 10:23; Acts 8:1; Romans 8:28; 1 Corinthians 1:17–31; 2 Corinthians 1:8–11; 4:7–12; 6:4–10; 12:7–10.

26. VOICE OF GOD (Children, Disobedience, God, Obedience, Prayer, Promises, Youth)

At the age of seven, James Ryle was put in an orphanage. His natural father was in prison, his stepfather was a violent alcoholic, and his mother couldn't cope. It was a grim place to be in, and not long after his arrival two boys ran away. They were caught a couple of days later, and James Ryle says,

'I can still remember the chilling sounds of their screams echoing through the halls as they were beaten for having done something so foolish. As I lay in my bed, I pulled the covers up about my face and timidly whispered a simple prayer to the God I did not know, but feared. "I promise, God," I said, "I'll never run away."'

As the years went by, James got tougher and more independent, and by the time he was fourteen he had

had enough of the orphanage. With two friends, he jumped the fence and ran away. And as they ran across the fields something happened which he really wasn't expecting. In his own words, 'The voice of the Lord spoke to me out of the silence, stopping me in my tracks: "You promised." That's all he said, but it was enough. I was dumbstruck. My first thought was, "I cannot believe that you would bring that up at a time like this!"'

That was the first time that James Ryle heard the voice of God. But he ignored it. After a moment's hesitation, he kept running. And he kept on running for the rest of his teenage years, running from his past, and running away from God. It wasn't until he ended up in prison that God spoke to him again. But that's another story.

Source: Adapted from James Ryle, Hippo in the Garden (Highland, 1992), pp 12–15.

Bible references: Genesis 3:9; 16:8; 22:11; Exodus 3:4; 1 Samuel 3:1–18; Psalm 32:8; Isaiah 30:21; Jeremiah 1:4–10; Amos 7:14–15; Acts 9:4; 10:13–15.

27. VOICE OF GOD (Art, Cathedrals, Church, Conversion, Faith, Peace, Presence of God, Salvation)

The sheer diversity of the ways in which people come to faith in Christ is quite amazing. Tony Morton rose to become one of the key leaders in the New Churches, based at Southampton Community Church and with apostolic oversight over some twenty other congregations. But his conversion was not what you might expect – and certainly not what he expected.

It was 1968, and Tony was a student home from college. He was depressed and desperate. He wandered into Liverpool's Anglican cathedral and walked into the Chapel of the Holy Spirit. At that moment the sun shone through a stained glass window which depicted Christ praying in the Garden of Gethsemane and Tony heard a voice speak to him, 'He died for you – just live for him.'

Suddenly he was filled with a wonderful warm sense of the presence and peace of God, and he walked out of the cathedral a new man. He didn't know any Christians yet, but he did know God, and his life was transformed there and then. That night when he went out with his mates he told them, 'I've become a Christian.' They laughed, but he knew it was true.

Source: Adapted from Brian Hewitt, Doing a New Thing? (Hodder & Stoughton, 1995), p 37.

Bible references: Exodus 3:4; 1 Samuel 3:1–18; Isaiah 30:21; Jeremiah 1:4–10; Amos 7:14–15; Acts 9:4; 10:13–15; 2 Corinthians 5:17.

HUMAN NATURE

28. BROKENNESS (Children, Divorce, Husbands, Marriage, Men, Parables, Relationships, Sin, Suffering, Wives, Women, the World)

A busy mother asked her husband to look after their little boy, just for half an hour, so that she could get on. He rather grudgingly agreed, but didn't really want to, because he had plans of his own. So he showed the boy a picture in a magazine, a map of the world, and said, 'Let's make our own jigsaw puzzle.' He took a pair of scissors, cut out the page, and then cut the picture up into lots of little squares. 'There,' he said to the boy, 'I'm just going to do a couple of things, and while I'm busy, see if you can put the picture back together again.'

He disappeared off into the next room but was astonished when only a few minutes later the boy called to him, 'Dad, I've finished.' 'You can't have done!' he said, but when he came back, he could see that the boy was absolutely right: he'd put the map back together in exactly the right order.

'How did you manage to do it so quickly?' the father asked. 'Well, you see,' the boy replied, 'When you cut the map out of the magazine I could see that on the back there was a picture of a man and a woman. And I thought to myself that if I could just put the man and the woman back together again, then I could put the world back together at the same time.'

Source: Adapted from J. John, New Wine 1998.

Bible references: John 10:16; 11:52; 13:34–35; 17:20–23; 1 Corinthians 12:12–13; 2 Corinthians 5:17–20; Galatians 3:28; Ephesians 2:14–16; Colossians 3:11.

29. CHALLENGE (Belief, Change, Conversion, Evangelism, Faith, Honesty, Lifestyle, Unbelief)

The American preacher Steve Brown once got into a conversation about the Christian faith with the sound engineer who'd been recording a radio interview he'd just given. Steve suddenly realised he had to be somewhere else, so he gave the engineer his card, and on the back wrote the names of a couple of Christian books which he thought the man would find helpful. He said, 'Call me after you've read these books, then we'll talk again.' The man thanked him, and Steve turned to go.

As he was walking out of the studio, the sound engineer called after him, 'Hey, Reverend! I don't think I'm going to read these books.'

'Why not?' Steve said, 'You're asking questions.'

'Yeah, you're right,' the man replied. 'But I don't want to read them. Because if I read them, I may find out you're right. And if you're right, I've got to change. But I don't want to change.'

Source: Adapted from Steve Brown, in A Voice in the Wilderness (Multnomah Press, 1993), pp 50–51.

Bible references: Matthew 19:16–22; Mark 10:17–30; Luke 14:28–33; 18:18–23; Acts 26:26–30.

30. CRITICISM (Dissatisfaction, Intolerance, Humour)

President Lyndon Johnson had the reputation of being incredibly critical. It is said that he once saw his press secretary's desk in a terrible mess and said, 'Kilduff, I hope your mind isn't as cluttered as your desk.' Naturally Kilduff made sure that the next time the President saw his desk, it was completely clear, with everything put away in the proper place. This time Lyndon Johnson said, 'Kilduff, I hope your brain isn't as vacant as your desk.'

Source: Adapted from Geoffrey Regan, Histrionics (Robson Books, 1994), p 172.

Bible references: Romans 15:2; 1 Corinthians 14:3; 1 Thessalonians 5:11; James 3:2–12.

31. EXCUSES (Blame, Character, Sin, Humour)

A panda walked into a restaurant and ordered a huge meal. He ate it with obvious enjoyment and then called a waiter. The waiter came to the table, thinking the panda wanted to pay, but the panda pulled out a gun and shot the waiter. Then he got up and walked out of the restaurant. The manager was horrified. He ran after the panda and shouted, 'What do you think you're doing? You can't just walk into my restaurant, eat a meal, shoot one of my waiters and then leave!'

'Oh yes, I can,' said the panda. 'In fact I have to. I can't help it. That's what pandas do.'

'What do you mean, that's what pandas do?' asked the manager.

'It's the way I'm made,' said the panda. 'Look it up: see for yourself.' And he walked off.

The manager went back into the restaurant, utterly confused. Look it up? he thought to himself. Look what up? Where? So he looked in the only place he could think of – the dictionary. And there he found the explanation:

'Panda: Asian mammal who eats shoots and leaves.'

Source: Adapted from Adrian Plass, Bible a Month Club Newsletter, July 1997.

Bible references: Genesis 3:12–13; Jeremiah 2:34–35; Romans 7:18–19; 1 Corinthians 10:13; Galatians 5:17; 1 John 1:8–10.

32. FORGIVENESS (Arrogance, Pride, Sin)

While he was in the United States, in Georgia, John Wesley served as chaplain to General Oglethorpe. One day the general said proudly to Wesley, 'I never forgive.'

'Then I hope, sir,' replied Wesley, 'that you never sin.'

Source: Adapted from Stephen Travis, I Believe in the Second Coming of Jesus (Hodder & Stoughton, 1988), p 192.

Bible references: Matthew 6:12–15; 18:21–35; Mark 11:25–26; Luke 6:37; John 20:23; Ephesians 4:32; Colossians 3:13; James 2:13; 1 John 1:8–10.

33. HUMILITY (Creation, God, Man, Pride)

US President Theodore Roosevelt used to go on camping trips with his friend the naturalist William Beebe. When they had struck camp for the night, the two men used to sit and gaze up at the stars, and in the vast expanse of the night sky they used to look for the constellation of Pegasus. Then they would locate a tiny pinprick of light next to it, and together they would say, 'That is the spiral galaxy in Andromeda. It is as large as our Milky Way. It is one of a hundred million galaxies. It consists of one hundred billion suns, each larger than our sun.' Then Roosevelt would say, 'Now I think we are small enough. Let's go to bed.'

Source: Adapted from John Ortberg in Dangers, Toils and Snares: Resisting the Hidden Temptations of Ministry (Multnomah Books, 1994), p 102.

Bible references: Job 25:2–6; 38; Psalms 8; 19:1–6; 104; 144:3–4; Isaiah 40:12–20; Romans 1:19–20.

34. MISTAKES (Experience, Gullibility, Sin, Stupidity, Humour)

A man once saw an advert in his local paper offering an amazing bargain: a luxury cruise for only £25. The ad instructed those who wanted to take up this fantastic offer to turn up at the docks at midnight the following Tuesday, with the fee in cash.

The man turned up at the quayside at midnight on the appointed day, but to his disappointment he couldn't see a cruise liner anywhere. The docks were dark and apparently deserted, and he was just about to leave when he heard footsteps behind him. He started to turn round, but then someone whacked him over the head, and he blacked out.

When he woke up, he found himself in broad daylight, floating in a rowing boat in the harbour. He had a big bump on the top of his head, and his wallet was gone. As he gingerly sat up, he saw another rowing boat in the water nearby, with a man lying in it with a bump on his head, too. So he called across, 'Do they serve breakfast on this cruise?'

'I don't think so,' the other man called back. 'At least, they didn't last year.'

Source: Adapted from James Ryle, New Wine, August 1997.

Bible references: Exodus 7–12; Proverbs 26:11; John 8:34; Romans 7:14–25; 2 Timothy 2:25–26; Hebrews 6:4–8; James 1:14–15; 2 Peter 2:20–22.

35. NAMES (Professions, Humour)

It is well known that Hebrew babies were given names that were meant to reflect their characters. In the Middle Ages lots of people in Europe were named after their profession: Smith, Butcher, Carter and so on. Although we don't do that any more, scientists suspect that people are attracted to professions which reflect their name, either consciously or not. So there are articles on 'Animal behaviour' by Lionel Tiger and Robin Fox, 'Effects of tactile stimulation' by someone called Finger, 'Responses to authoritarian discipline' by Stern and Cope, 'Juvenile Delinquency' by Lively and Reckless, and 'Effects of parental pressure on school performance' by someone called Mumpower.

There's also a paper on incontinence by J. W. Splatt and D. Weedon, John Barnacle is an expert on marine timber and Professor Solt an expert on water desalinisation. Daniel Snowman wrote a book about the North Pole, J. Lust is a sex therapist, Laura Slaughter specialises in impulsive aggression at the University of Texas, J. Angst is an expert on depression, and P.J. Coffer is a clinician in lung disease in the Netherlands.

There are also countless examples outside the academic world, such as B. Woof the dog show judge in New South Wales, W. Iball, a senior nurse at St Paul's Eye Unit in Liverpool, or Grant Warmbath, a hotel manager in Scotland. The Ecclesiastical Insurance Company employ a Mrs Sue Heaven. Hampton School in Hertfordshire has Miss Beat the music teacher and Mr Sentance in the English department. The Meteorological Office employs a Flood and a Frost, their counterparts in Seattle have Dave Storm, and in Australia the Bureau of Meteorology employs A. Rainbow. Finally, Katherine Shelfer writes books for librarians, Neil Gamble is the head of Sydney Casino, and a member of the Metropolitan Police indecent publications squad is called Richard Vice.

Source: Adapted from New Scientist, 25 April 1998, and The Daily Telegraph, 27 April 1998.

Bible references: Genesis 17:5,15; 25:25–26; 29:32 – 30:24; 35:10; Judges 6:32; Ruth 1:20; Isaiah 7:3,14; 8:1; Jeremiah 20:3; Hosea 1:4–9; Matthew 1:21,23.

36. POWER (Arrogance, Man, Pride, Royalty, Sea voyages, Storms, Weather, Humour)

Queen Victoria was once going across to Ireland in the royal yacht when the ship ran into some very rough weather. A huge wave made the ship lurch to one side, almost knocking the queen off her feet. She immediately sent an attendant to the bridge with the command, 'Give the captain my compliments, and tell him that he's not to let that happen again!'

Source: Adapted from Geoffrey Regan, Histrionics (Robson Books, 1994), p 27.

Bible references: Job 38:8–11; Psalm 107:23–28; Proverbs 16:18; Ezekiel 27:25 – 28:2; Jonah 1:4–15; Matthew 8:23–27; Mark 4:35–41; Luke 8:22–25.

37. PRIDE (Arrogance, Boasting, Patriotism, Tourism, Humour)

A Texan was once visiting a sheep farm in Australia. The farmer showed him the house, 'It's a fine old colonial building,' he said proudly, 'built in the 1880s. In fact it's the oldest in these parts.' 'It's a mighty fine little cottage,' replied the Texan. 'Not dissimilar from my home, in fact, though that was built in the 1850s, and is, oh, I suppose about twice the size.'

'Can I take you down to the shearing sheds?' said the Australian. 'We're rather proud of them – we can shear thirty-five sheep an hour down there.' 'That's a good number,' replied the Texan. 'Why, back home we only manage to shear fifty an hour!'

The Australian gritted his teeth and managed not to comment. But then he had a better idea. 'Tell you what, mate,' he said, 'Why don't I give you a tour of the farm? We'll have to go by helicopter, of course: it's too big to see on the ground. We've got 5,000 head of sheep here.'

'Why, that would be just grand,' the Texan answered. 'Of course back home we have to use a plane to see our ranch. We've got 10,000 sheep on our little spread.'

They flew over the farm and had just landed beside the farmhouse when a kangaroo bounced past. 'What the heck was that?' the Texan exclaimed. The farmer was a quick thinker. 'Don't you have grasshoppers in Texas?'

Source: Adapted from Steve Williams, 1980.

Bible references: Psalm 10; Proverbs 13:10; 16:18; 21:24; Romans 12:3,16; 1 Corinthians 3:18–20; Galatians 6:3–5.

38. REMEMBRANCE (Army, Death, Epitaphs, Fame, First World War, Immortality, Life, Reputation, Sacrifice, War)

The American writer Will Willimon was once travelling through southern England when his car broke down. While he was waiting for it to be repaired, he wandered round the village churchyard, where he came across a plot of some fifty graves surrounded by a low brick wall. The plot was nearly choked with grass, but on the wall above there was a large granite slab, which proclaimed in bold letters: 'WE SHALL NEVER FORGET YOUR SACRIFICE.'

Intrigued by this, Will Willimon looked at the graves more carefully, and found that they were all of young men from New Zealand aged between seventeen and twenty-five. But who were they, and why were so many of them buried in this English churchyard, so far from home? He couldn't find any clues in the churchyard or the church, so he asked at the local museum. The attendant there had no idea who the young men were, nor had anyone else in the village that Willimon asked. He himself guessed that they had been soldiers stationed nearby during World War I, who had died during the flu epidemic of 1918.

But this was the point that struck him so forcibly: the impressive inscription set in granite was an empty promise; in fact it was a downright lie. Their sacrifice *had* been forgotten. No one remembered them any more.

Source: Adapted from Will Willimon in Preaching magazine, March/April 1997.

Bible references: Job 7:6–10; 14:1–2; Psalms 39:4–6; 49; 90:3–12; 103:15–16; 144:3–4; Ecclesiastes 1:11; 2:15–16; Isaiah 40:7–8.

39. SELF-ESTEEM (Arrogance, Commandments, Community, Condescension, Outsiders, Prejudice, Pride)

In 1933 the Danish writer Aksel Sandemose wrote a novel called *A Refugee Crosses the Tracks,* set in an imaginary town called Jante. The people of Jante have a way of cutting people down to size, summed up in the Jante Law ('Janteloven'), their own ten commandments. You may recognise the mentality behind them.

1. Do not think you are special.
2. Do not think that you are as good as us.
3. Do not think that you are cleverer than us.
4. Do not imagine that you are better than us.
5. Do not think that you know more than us.
6. Do not think that you are more important than us.
7. Do not think that you are good at anything.
8. Do not laugh at us.
9. Do not think that anyone cares about you.
10. Do not think that you can teach us anything.

Source: Simon Coupland, with thanks to Marit Mundahl Haslestad.

Bible references: Psalm 73; Isaiah 29:14–16; Matthew 11:25–26; Luke 10:21; John 7:45–49; 9:24–34,39–41; 1 Corinthians 1:25–31.

40. TEMPTATION (Desire, Devil, Discipleship, Lust, Sin, Spiritual warfare)

A young man once went to see the great German preacher Martin Luther to ask his advice. He said that he was constantly plagued by wrongful desires and lustful thoughts, and didn't know what to do. Luther's reply was typically blunt, 'You can't stop the birds flying to and fro in the air,' he said, 'but you can certainly stop them nesting in your hair!'

Source: Translated from Martin Luther, Tischreden, no. 7075.

Bible references: Matthew 4:3–11; Luke 4:1–13; Ephesians 4:27; 6:11–12; James 4:7; 1 Peter 5:8–10.

FORGIVENESS AND UNFORGIVENESS

41. CHANGE (Conversion, the Cross, Discipleship, Families, Forgiveness, God, Jesus, Prayer, Prison, Repentance, Salvation, Terrorism, Violence, Voice of God)

David 'Packie' Hamilton was a loyalist terrorist who came to Christian faith while he was serving an eleven-year prison sentence in Northern Ireland. Shortly afterwards he found out that another man had moved in with his wife. That was bad enough. But worse was to follow. He discovered that during a row, the boyfriend had punched David's three-year-old son in the face, smashing his nose and leaving him with a stutter. It's easy to imagine the strain this put on David's new-found faith. He told God that if this man ever ended up in jail with him, he would give up being a Christian and kill him.

Three years later the opportunity came. David was getting some hot water for a cup of tea when he saw the man in a cell across the landing. The other guy immediately pulled his cell door shut, which automatically locked it: obviously he realised that he'd been spotted. But David knew that his chance would come.

A few days later he was cutting the grass when he saw the man walking towards him, accompanied by a prison officer. 'Punched any babies lately?' David sneered. 'It was an accident,' the man said, but David didn't believe him. 'I'm going to kill you,' he vowed. An inmate who was gardening with David couldn't believe it. 'You're a Christian, and you just said you're going to kill that man?' he asked. 'You don't know what he did to my baby,' David replied.

Over the next few weeks David watched and waited for the right time to make a move. He tried to psyche himself up, to get rid of all other emotions and concentrate solely on the desire to kill this man. He organised a distraction in the prison yard to draw the guards away. He was pacing up and down in his cell, waiting for the door to be opened, when God spoke clearly in his mind, 'David, forgive him.' 'I'll forgive him after I've killed him,' David said, and kept on walking. Again the words came into his head, 'David, forgive him.' So this time he said, 'I won't kill him, but I want to beat him badly. It's only right; he deserves it.' But all he could hear echoing round his head were the words, 'David, forgive him.'

David Hamilton goes on: 'So I got angry with God, stopped walking, looked up and shouted, "Look what he did to my son!" It was then God spoke to me again and said, "Look what they did to my Son!" I fell to my knees and wept and I asked God to help me forgive him. I came up from my knees a different man.'

'I went out into the yard where I saw him standing under the shelter. He was afraid. He reminded me of a scared rabbit caught in car headlights. As I walked towards him he didn't move. I stopped just a few feet from him, looked into his eyes and saw the fear. I could easily have taken his life at that moment. Instead I said, "I am a Christian now; God has forgiven me and I forgive you for what you did to my son. You can stay in the yard, no one will harm you."'

'That day was a turning point in my life. I knew then I would never go back to my old life, or back to the Organisation again. I would never hold a gun or plant another bomb as long as I would live. From that day on I have never doubted my salvation because I know the power of God to change a person.'

Source: Adapted from David T. Hamilton, A Cause Worth Living For (Highland Books, 1997), reproduced in Renewal, February 1998.

Bible references: Proverbs 20:22; Matthew 5:38–48; 6:12–15; 18:21–35; Mark 11:25–26; Luke 6:27–37; 11:4; 17:3–4; John 20:23; Romans 12:17–21; 1 Corinthians 13:5; Ephesians 4:32; Colossians 3:13; 1 Thessalonians 5:15; 1 Peter 3:8–9.

42. CLEANSING (Atonement, Baptism, the Cross, Forgiveness, Guilt, Jesus, John the Baptist, Repentance, Salvation, Sin)

John the Baptist is baptising in the river Jordan, and huge crowds are coming to him, and it is all rather disorganised. So some businessmen in the crowd decide to sort things out and tidy things up. They set up tables and get people into queues and as each person reaches the front of the queue they are asked for their name, which is written on a sticky label. Then the person behind the desk asks what their main sin is, what it is that they want to be forgiven for. So Bob walks up to the table. 'What's your name?'

'Bob.'

'What's your most awful sin, Bob?'

'I stole some money from my boss.' So the person at the table writes in big letters BOB – EMBEZZLER on the label, and sticks it on Bob's chest.

The next person comes forward. 'What's your name?'

'Mary.'

'Mary, what's your worst sin?'

'I gossiped about some people. It wasn't so bad, what I said, but I know I shouldn't have done.'

So they write down MARY – GOSSIP and stick it on her.

Another man walks up to the table. 'Name?'

'George.'

'George, what's your sin?'

'I've often thought about how much I'd like to have my neighbour's car.'

So they write down GEORGE – COVETER and stick it on him.

Another man comes up. 'What's your name?'

'Gordon.'

'What have you done, Gordon?'

'I had an affair.'

So they write down GORDON – ADULTERER, and slap the label on his chest.

Then Jesus comes to be baptised. He hasn't got a label on his chest. But he walks down the line of people waiting to be baptised and one by one, he peels the labels off their chests and sticks them on himself. Then he goes to John, and as he steps down into the water, the river washes away the writing from every single one of those labels.

Source: Adapted from Gordon MacDonald, quoted in Haddon Robinson, in A Voice in the Wilderness (Multnomah Press, 1993), pp 77–78.

Bible references: Psalms 32:1–2; 51; 103:8–12; Isaiah 1:18; 43:25; 53:4–6; Ezekiel 36:25–27; Matthew 3:1–17; Mark 1:4–11; Luke 3:1–22; John 1:19–34; 3:16–18; Romans 8:1–2; 1 Corinthians 6:11; 2 Corinthians 5:17–20; Ephesians 2:1–5; Hebrews 9:13–14; 10:11–22; 1 John 1:7–9.

43. CONFESSION (Absolution, Accidents, Addiction, Adultery, Affairs, Alcohol, Apology, Conscience, Forgiveness, Guilt, Modern life, Repentance, Sin)

People need to say sorry. If proof of that were needed, it's provided by the popularity of a telephone answering service in Los Angeles called the Apology Sound-Off Line. People ring the number and then have sixty seconds to make their confession in the freedom offered by total anonymity. The service is proving remarkably popular, with an average of two hundred callers every day. Many people ring to admit that they've committed adultery. Some confess to criminal acts, including rape, child abuse and even murder, all secure in the knowledge that their call won't be traced. An alcoholic rings to apologise to all the people hurt during eighteen years of addiction. A young woman phones to confess that she's just been in a car crash in which five people died. 'I just want to say I'm sorry,' she sobs. 'I wish I could bring them back.' Yes, people need to say sorry. But how much better it would be if someone could offer them forgiveness.

Source: Adapted from Philip Yancey, What's So Amazing about Grace? (Zondervan, 1997), p 35.

Bible references: Leviticus 26:40–42; 1 Samuel 7:6; Nehemiah 1:5–7; 9:1–3; Psalms 32; 51; Proverbs 28:13; Isaiah 59:12–13; Daniel 9:4–6; James 5:16; 1 John 1:8–10.

44. FORGIVENESS (Baptism, Change, Cleansing, God, Repentance)

In one of C.S. Lewis's children's books about Narnia, *The Voyage of the Dawn Treader*, there is a boy called Eustace. He's a rather nasty boy, so nasty in fact that he turns into a dragon. But then he comes to his senses and longs to be a boy again. The trouble is, he doesn't know how. He tries to scratch off his skin with his claws, like a snake sloughing off its skin, but every time he manages to peel off a layer of scales, there's another layer underneath. And then the lion, Aslan, says, 'You will have to let me undress you.' Eustace is afraid, but he has no other option. So he lets Aslan remove the dragon skin. Afterwards he said

> The very first tear he made was so deep that I thought it had gone right into my heart. And when he began pulling the skin off, it hurt worse than anything I've ever felt. The only thing that made me able to bear it was just the pleasure of feeling the stuff peel off....
>
> Well, he peeled the beastly stuff right off – just as I thought I'd done it myself the other three times, only they hadn't hurt – and there it was lying on the grass... And there was I as smooth and soft as a peeled switch and smaller than I had been. Then he caught hold of me... and threw me into the water. It smarted like anything but only for a moment. After that it became perfectly delicious and as soon as I started swimming and splashing I found that all the pain had gone.... And then I saw why. I'd turned into a boy again.

Source: Adapted from C.S. Lewis, The Voyage of the Dawn Treader (Fontana, 1980), pp 86–87.

Bible references: Psalms 32:1–2; 51; 103:8–12; Isaiah 1:18; 53:4–6; Ezekiel 36:25–27; John 3:16–18; Romans 8:1–2; 1 Corinthians 6:11; 2 Corinthians 5:17–20; Ephesians 2:1–5; Hebrews 9:13–14; 10:11–22; 1 John 1:7–9.

45. GRACE (Atonement, Change, Church, Conversion, the Cross, Discipleship, Jesus, Lifestyle, Love, Prison)

The former Watergate conspirator Charles Colson works tirelessly for the Prison Fellowship, trying to bring the love of Jesus to those who are behind bars. In a prison in Brazil he found a powerful example of the difference Christ can make. Humaita Prison in San Jose dos Campos houses 350 offenders, and for many years it has been run not by the state but by Christian volunteers.

The ethos of the prison is summed up by the words which are said to a prisoner when he enters the maximum security wing and his handcuffs are removed: 'In this prison your heart is handcuffed by love and you are watched over by Christ.' And these are not just pious words: the prison's success rate in transforming the inmates' lives is remarkable. The recidivism rate for Brazilian prisons is about the world average: seventy-five per cent. From Humaita, out of five hundred prisoners released over eighteen years, only twenty-one reoffended: four per cent.

Colson says:

> The secret of the prison is found in a small cell in the high security area, the notorious punishment cell. In years past, prisoners had been thrown into it naked, served one meagre meal each day, and sometimes were so crowded on top of one another that they suffocated. But we were told there was now only one prisoner in the cell.
>
> My stomach tightened as the door swung open. As I entered I saw fresh flowers, an altar and a central crucifix, with a banner proclaiming *Estamos Juntos*: We are together. The prisoner in that solitary

cell was Jesus, his cross a vivid reminder that he had served the sentence for all in that prison, and that he was with them still.

Those inmates, poor and without privilege, live with a richer sense of God's grace than I've felt in many an ornate church building.

Source: Adapted from Renewal, June 1991.

Bible references: Psalm 32:1–2; Isaiah 43:25; 53:4–7; John 3:14–17; Romans 4:25; 5:6–11; 8:1–4; 2 Corinthians 5:14–21; 1 Peter 1:18–19; 2:9–12,24–25; 3:18.

46. LOVE (Communism, Evangelism, Faith, Hardship, Intercession, Persecution, Prayer, Reconciliation, Suffering, Torture, Witness)

Paul Negrut, President of the Romanian Evangelical Alliance, tells of a man who spent seventeen years in Communist prisons for his faith. One evening Paul went to see him, and arrived just after the secret police had left. There was blood all over the man's face, and Paul was filled with anger, but his friend said, 'We are not here to complain, Paul. We are here to praise our Lord. Let's pray.' So they knelt down together, and Paul was so angry that he didn't really know what to pray, but his friend more than made up for it. He prayed for the secret police, for the Communist party, for those who had beaten him up. He asked God's forgiveness for them, God's blessing on them, and God's love to be poured out upon their families. Paul Negrut says, 'I never heard somebody praying for his enemies with such love as that man.'

After they had prayed his friend said that the secret police came twice every week to torture him, and that every time that they came he looked into the eyes of the secret policeman and told him that he loved him. And he said to him, 'Sir, if we see each other before the throne of judgement, and if you are eternally lost, I want you to know that it is not because I hate you. It will be because you rejected Jesus' love and my love.'

Some time later the policeman came back to the house on his own. This time it wasn't to beat the man up. It was to say that he had become a Christian. He said, 'Your love melted my heart and through your love I saw Jesus' love, and I came to know Jesus.' He explained that he had found out he had cancer, and only had a few more weeks to live. He came to ask forgiveness. He came to pray with the man he had tortured.

Source: Adapted from UK Focus, November 1996.

Bible references: Proverbs 20:22; Song of Songs 8:6–7; Matthew 5:10–12,38–48; Luke 6:22–23; John 15:18–25; Romans 8:35–39; 2 Corinthians 1:3–11; 4:7–12; 6:4–10; Philippians 1:27–30; 1 Peter 3:14–17; 4:12–16.

47. PEACE (Absolution, Apology, Confession, Conscience, Forgiveness, Guilt, Reconciliation, Suffering, War)

Every so often a picture captures the attention of the world. In 1972 it happened with an image from the Vietnam war, showing a young Vietnamese girl running towards the camera, tears streaming down her face, her clothes blown off by the American bombs which had destroyed her village. The sky behind her is full of smoke from the fire. Soldiers with guns walk behind her, apparently unmoved. Many people can picture that photograph in their mind's eye just by hearing it described.

John Plummer was one of the helicopter pilots who helped organise the attack. Like so many others, he, too, was shocked by that picture, and over the next twenty-four years it haunted him. He longed to be able to find the girl, if she was still alive, and to say that he was sorry for what he had done. But how could he? He was a Methodist pastor in Virginia in the United States, and he didn't even know her name.

Friends tried to convince him that he had no need to feel guilty. After all, he had tried to make sure that there were no civilians in the village when the napalm was dropped. But his conscience still tormented him, and his guilt helped to break up his marriage and drive him to drink.

Then on Veterans' Day in 1996, he went to the Vietnam memorial in Washington with a group of fellow pilots to try and make their peace with the past. To his amazement, a woman spoke who identified herself as the girl in the picture. Her name was Phan Thi Kim Phuc, and she had come to say that she was not bitter, that even though she still suffered from the burns she had received that day, she forgave the men who had bombed her village, and wanted only peace.

Afterwards John was able to speak to her, just for a couple of minutes, and all he could say was 'I'm sorry, I'm sorry,' over and over again. She put her arms around him and said, 'It's all right. I forgive you.'

At last, John says, he can put the past behind him. The nightmare is over. He is at peace.

Source: Adapted from Johann Christoph Arnold, The Lost Art of Forgiving, reproduced in Renewal, May 1998.

Bible references: Psalms 32:1–2; 51:3; Proverbs 28:13; Matthew 5:23–24; James 5:16.

48. PRIDE (Arguments, Bitterness, Church, Clergy, Committees, Disagreement, Division, Forgiveness, Grace, Grudges, Ministry, Music, Organ music, PCCs, Prayer, Preaching, Quarrels, Reconciliation, Sin, Stubbornness, Unforgiveness)

In the United States there is one poor pastor who for eleven years preached to a man who sat through the entire service with his fingers in his ears. What happened was this. Eleven years earlier the church committee had discussed whether they should put in a new sound system. The man had opposed it. When the decision was taken to go ahead anyway, he decided to make his protest obvious. So week by week he sat in church with his fingers in his ears, just to make it clear to everyone that he still wasn't happy with the decision.

The writer Calvin Miller tells of a lady in his own congregation who disagreed with the rest of the church music committee over which organ to buy. Everyone else was in agreement, and so Calvin Miller, as the pastor, went along with them. But this lady would have none of it. And so for four years she shunned the pastor at church, she gossiped about him among her friends, and she cut him dead if they happened to meet in the street.

Then one day a visiting preacher challenged the congregation to go and pray with anyone that they needed to be reconciled with. Calvin Miller approached the lady and asked her if she would forgive him and if they could pray together. She said, 'Pastor, I could never pray with you. Remember, I wanted a Rogers organ and you chose to stand against me. In fact, I feel uncomfortable that you've come to me in this service to call attention to me by letting others see me refuse you.' Even so, he prayed for her, he gave thanks for her and asked God's blessing on her. But, he says, 'When I rose from the pew, she still had that firm, hard look that still characterises her wintry expression in church.'

Source: Adapted from Calvin Miller, Disarming the Darkness (Zondervan, 1998), pp 34–36.

Bible references: Matthew 6:12–15; 18:21–35; Mark 11:25–26; Luke 6:36–37; 17:3–4; Ephesians 4:2–3,29–32; Philippians 2:3–5,14–15; Colossians 3:12–14; Hebrews 12:14–15; James 2:13; 5:9; 2 Peter 1:5–11; 1 John 2:9–11; Jude 16.

49. RECONCILIATION (Apology, Bigotry, Change, Conversion, Forgiveness, Hatred, Hope, Love, Peace, Prison, Repentance, Salvation, Sin, Terrorism, Testimony, Violence, Voice of God, War)

In 1975 the IRA inmates in Long Kesh jail in Northern Ireland burned it down. For a night they went on the rampage before the British Army regained control. Tom Kelly was one of the IRA internees in the camp that night. James Tate was imprisoned there, too, but on the opposite side, as an Ulster Volunteer Force commander. Twenty years later, they find themselves working together for peace and reconciliation in Ulster, transformed by the love of Christ.

James Tate helped to found the Ulster Volunteer Force in the staunchly Loyalist Sandy Row area of Belfast. He was arrested one Easter Sunday morning in possession of guns and ammunition, and served six years in prison, during which time he became a commander over eighty men. Tom Kelly was drawn into the IRA as a teenager. He started off stripping down weapons, then became a fully fledged volunteer. He, too, was found guilty of possession of weapons, and sentenced to seven years in the notorious H-blocks. He took part in the so-called blanket protest, when prisoners refused to wear clothes, and the 'dirty protest', when inmates fouled their cells. Friends of his died in the hunger strikes.

While they were in prison, both James and Tom separately saw that violence would not achieve anything. James left the UVF, despite being threatened, and eventually found work doing odd jobs at a Belfast mission. While he was there, he was impressed by the practical Christian love that he saw. What finally brought him to faith was hearing Nicky Cruz, the former New York gangster, say at a meeting that God would not only forgive our sins, but also forget them. That was now what James desperately wanted.

On his release from prison, Tom Kelly ran a club for the IRA, but he too was disillusioned, and wanted out. In his case, God intervened in a dramatic way. At a Christian meeting which his wife had taken him along to, he heard God say to him, 'Tom, let me have your heart.' He said, 'If it's you, God, you can take it, because I don't like it.' And he, too, became a Christian.

When the two men met some years later, they realised that God had brought them together to show that he can bring forgiveness and healing even in the darkest places. Now they speak together across the divide, asking for forgiveness, and promoting peace and reconciliation, As Tom puts it, they want to show that reconciliation isn't a myth, but a reality. God has given them a message of hope in place of despair, to show people love rather than hatred. He has turned them from being men of war to men of peace.

Source: Simon Coupland.

Bible references: Psalm 133; Isaiah 9:6; John 10:16; 13:34–35; 17:20–23; 1 Corinthians 12:13; 2 Corinthians 5:17–21; Galatians 3:26–28; Ephesians 2:1–10,13–17; Colossians 2:13–15; 3:11–15.

50. REPENTANCE (Apology, Confession, Conscience, Crime, Guilt, Obedience, Preaching, Restitution, Sin, Witness)

Maurice Pritchard, the traffic administrator of the Midland Red bus company in Shrewsbury, was going through the post one morning when he was surprised to find a letter with a £5 note in it. The woman who had sent it explained that as a child, some twenty years earlier, she had sometimes avoided paying the bus fare on her way home from school. Her letter went on, 'In church on Sunday our pastor preached about restitution for things we had done wrong, and I remembered. I wanted to apologise to you and honour God by paying what I owe. I think the same bus fare would cost 50p now, hence the £5 enclosed.' Mr Pritchard told his local paper, the *Shrewsbury Chronicle*, 'We were all astonished by the letter. It's such a shame we weren't able to thank the woman, because although she had signed it, the signature was virtually unreadable.'

Source: Adapted from The Daily Telegraph, 14 June 1997.

Bible references: Exodus 22:1–15; Leviticus 6:1–5; Numbers 5:5–7; Matthew 5:23–24; Luke 3:8; 16:9; 19:1–10.

51. REVENGE (Grudges, Hatred, Hijacking, Murder, Sin, Unforgiveness, Violence)

In 1987 a Pacific South West Airlines aircraft with forty-eight people on board crashed in California. Flight investigators found a gun in the wreckage, and from skin found on the trigger were able to piece together the tragedy that had destroyed the plane.

Fingerprint experts discovered that the gun had been held by David Burke, a former flight attendant who had been sacked by the airline for stealing $69.

Burke had held onto his security pass, which was how he had managed to get on the plane carrying a gun. The cockpit voice recorder showed that Burke had gone up to his former boss, Ray Thompson, who was also on the flight.

Burke said, 'Hi, Ray. I think it's sort of ironical that we end up like this. I asked for leniency for my family, remember? Well I got none and you'll get none.' He then shot Thompson, walked up to the cockpit and killed the crew as well. The plane nose-dived to the ground, and all forty-eight people on board were killed.

Source: Channel Four, Black Box, reviewed in The Times, 23 July 1998.

Bible references: Matthew 6:12–15; 18:21–35; Mark 11:25–26; Luke 6:36–37; 17:3–4; Ephesians 4:32; Colossians 3:13; James 2:13; 1 John 1:8–10.

52. REVENGE (Books, Curses, Forgiveness, Magic, Murder, Reconciliation, Stress, Theology, Torture, Unforgiveness, Voodoo, Witchcraft)

Sister Margaret Magdalen describes how she was visiting a book shop in South Africa, 'a very reputable bookshop', and was browsing through the books in the theology section, 'when I came upon a pile of books containing DIY voodoo kits. Each contained a little rubber effigy, a row of pins with coloured glass heads, and a book of curses and spells. On the lid of each box was a picture of a very hostile crowd with ugly expressions, shaking their fists and clearly hurling abuse at an identical effigy stuck all over with pins just like a cushion.'

'At the bottom of the box it read, "Revenge therapy for the over-stressed."'

What a contrast, she says, with the elderly lady who came before the Truth and Reconciliation Commission, who when Archbishop Desmond Tutu asked her, 'What do you want the Commission to do for you?', answered, 'I want you to find the person or persons who tortured my husband and who murdered my son, so that I can look them in the eye and say, "I forgive you."'

Source: Adapted from Renewal, May 1998.

Bible references: Matthew 6:12–15; 18:21–35; Mark 11:25–26; Luke 6:36–37; 17:3–4; Ephesians 4:32; Colossians 3:13; James 2:13; 1 John 1:8–10.

53. SIN (Absolution, Cleansing, Conscience, Confession, Cosmetics, Forgiveness, Guilt, Human nature, Perfume, Humour)

I am dousing myself with cosmetics
To stop me from smelling quite strong:
Max Factor, Gillette,
I've tried them all, yet
I'm convinced that something is wrong.
I go into Boots every Wednesday –
The assistants are ever so nice –
And there I buy Brut
To make me feel cute
And to help to kill the lice.
Yet still I'm convinced that something is wrong.
I even tried Vim,
My future looks dim,
'Cos now I just foam when it rains.
So, dear Estée Lauder, do tell me:
when my hair is all dyed
And I'm full of spice

Is it a phase?
Please help me erase
the sweat stain that lies deep inside.

Source: J. John, New Wine 1998.

Bible references: Psalm 51; Jeremiah 2:22; Ezekiel 36:25–27; 1 Corinthians 6:11; Hebrews 9:13–14; 10:21–22; 1 John 1:7–9.

54. UNFORGIVENESS (Absolution, Apology, Concentration camps, Confession, Conscience, Death, Evil, God, Guilt, Holocaust, Jews, Mercy, Murder, Nazism, Peace, Second World War, Suffering)

Simon Wiesenthal suffered terribly at the hands of the Nazis. Incredibly he survived years in Nazi concentration camps. He even survived the death block at Mauthausen, loading corpses into the crematoria. And from all the terrible images he witnessed during that time, one particular encounter went on haunting him long after the war.

It was in Poland in 1943. Wiesenthal was in a labour camp near Lemberg, the town where he had lived before the war, and where the Nazis were now gradually exterminating the Jewish population. Just five weeks earlier his own mother had been dragged out of her house in the Ghetto and driven away to certain death.

On this particular day he was on a work party taken to work at a military hospital in the town. A nurse beckoned him aside. 'Are you a Jew?' she asked. When he acknowledged that he was, she led him into the hospital, to a room where a man lay alone, wrapped in bandages, close to death.

As the nurse stood guard outside the door, the

wounded man told his story. His name was Karl. He was twenty-one. And he knew that he was dying. But he had something terrible on his conscience, something he needed to confess – to a Jew.

Karl had been a volunteer in the SS. He had fought on the Russian front. And in a town abandoned by the retreating Soviets, a booby-trapped house had exploded, killing thirty of his fellow soldiers. In reprisal Karl's unit had forced three hundred Jews into a house, and set the house alight. Any who escaped from the windows they shot.

Karl said:

> I don't know how many tried to jump out of the windows, but one family I shall never forget – least of all the child. It had black hair and dark eyes… And all the time I have been lying here I have never stopped thinking of [that] horrible deed… The pains in my body are terrible, but worst still is my conscience. It never ceases to remind me of the burning house and the family that jumped from the window.
>
> I know that what I have told you is terrible. In the long nights while I have been waiting for death, time and time again I have longed to talk about it to a Jew and beg forgiveness from him… I know that what I am asking is almost too much for you, but without your answer I cannot die in peace.

The room fell silent. Without a word, Simon Wiesenthal got up and left the room. And from that moment on he was haunted by the question: did he do the right thing? Should he, could he have offered forgiveness? His account ends with an appeal to the reader, 'Ask yourself the crucial question, "What would I have done?"'

Source: Adapted from Simon Wiesenthal, The Sunflower (W.H. Allen, 1970).

Bible references: Nehemiah 4:5; Psalms 69:27–28; 109:6–15; Isaiah 2:9; Jeremiah 18:23; Matthew 6:12–15; 18:21–35; Mark 11:25–26; Luke 6:36–37; 17:3–4; 24:34; Acts 7:60; Ephesians 4:32; Colossians 3:13; James 2:13; 1 John 1:8–10.

LOVE AND MARRIAGE

55. AFFAIRS (Adultery, Afterlife, Confession, Excuses, Heaven, Husbands, Judgement, Marriage, Revenge, Sin, Wives, Humour)

A man is convinced that his wife is having an affair, and he's getting really angry about it. So one day he leaves work early with the intention of catching her with her lover. He drives home to their apartment, which is a flat on the sixth floor, and as he stands outside the door with his key in his hand, he can smell cigar smoke. 'Right!' he thinks, and bursts open the door. But there's nobody in the sitting room, no one in the bathroom, just his wife on her own in the bedroom, and – the last place he looks – nobody in the kitchen. But then, from the open kitchen window, he hears the sound of a sports car starting up below. He looks down and sees a man who's parked right beside the bottom of the fire escape. His rage erupts. He is going to make this man pay! And immediately he sees the fridge standing next to the kitchen window. He drags it across to the window, lifts it to the sill, and pushes it down onto the sports car. Unfortunately for him, as the fridge falls out of the window, the cord with the plug on it wraps itself around his leg, and pulls him with it down onto the street below. Smack! End of act one.

Shortly afterwards, in heaven, St Peter is greeting the new arrivals. 'So why do you think we should let you in?' he asks the first man. 'I was just trying to save my marriage,' the man sobs. 'I loved her so much. It seemed the only way! And when I saw the fridge standing there.... ' 'There, there,' replies St Peter. 'We know all about the pain of betrayal and undeserved suffering. You just wait there and I'll come back to you in a minute.'

He turns to the next man. 'And what about you?' 'Well,' says the man, 'I had just bought a paper from the newsagent's and I was getting into my car when all of a sudden, out of the blue, this fridge falls out of the sky and lands on my head!' 'I see,' says Peter. 'Yes, we know all about the innocent bystander, too. Just wait here a minute and I'll get back to you as well.'

He turns to the third man. 'And tell me,' he says, 'What were you doing inside the fridge?'

Source: Adapted from J. John, New Wine 1998.

Bible references: Exodus 20:14; Deuteronomy 5:18; Proverbs 6:32–34; Matthew 5:27–30; James 2:11.

56. COMMITMENT (Hugs, Husbands, Intimacy, Love, Marriage, Old age, Sex, Wives, Humour)

An elderly married couple were lying in bed one night when the wife said softly to the husband, 'Do you remember how when we first married you always used to hold my hand in bed?'

'Yes,' he said, 'I do.' And in the darkness, under the covers, his gnarled old hand reached out and took hers.

'And do you remember how then you used to snuggle up to me and keep me warm on a cold night like tonight?'

'Yes,' he said, 'I do.' And in the darkness, under the covers, he grunted and groaned as he twisted his body to where she was lying, and cuddled up next to her.

'And do you remember how then you used to nibble my ear?'

'Yes,' he said with a sigh, turned back the covers and started to get out of bed.

'Where are you going?' the wife asked.

'To get my teeth.'

Source: Adapted from John Ortberg, The Life You've Always Wanted (Zondervan, 1997), pp 206–207.

Bible references: Song of Songs 2:6; 8:3,6–7; 1 Corinthians 13:4–7; Ephesians 5:25–33; Colossians 3:19; 1 Peter 3:7.

57. CONFLICT (Arguments, Counselling, Divorce, Husbands, Marriage, Quarrels, Reconciliation, Relationships, Remarriage, Wives, Humour)

Dallas and Irene Sherman of Cincinnati had a really stormy relationship. During one of their rows she deliberately wrecked two of their cars, which was the last straw for Dallas, and he filed for divorce. But as time went by, he found he couldn't live without her, so they were reconciled and actually got married again. Unfortunately they were soon back arguing again, only this time Irene shot Dallas in the hand and in the chest – twice. She was put on probation, he recovered, and divorced her again. But they still went on seeing each other, and during one of their attempts to get back together Irene shot Dallas again. He evidently didn't mind too much, as they were married for the third time in 1977.

Source: Adapted from Bill Bryson, Bizarre World (Warner Books, 1995), p 119.

Bible references: 1 Corinthians 13:4–7; Ephesians 4:26–27,31–32; 5:21–33; Colossians 3:18–19; James 1:19–20; 1 Peter 3:1–9.

58. CONFLICT (Arguments, History, Husbands, Marriage, Middle Ages, Quarrels, Wives, Humour)

In the University Library in Cambridge there is an old, leather-bound book containing illustrations copied from medieval manuscripts. There are no captions to the pictures, making them like early cartoon strips, but it isn't hard to work out what's going on. At the beginning of one story a woman is standing holding a club, with her skirt for some reason sewn together between her legs. Next to her, a man is standing in a barrel, with one hand behind his back. Battle then commences. The woman clouts the man, while the man tries to grab the woman. In the end she ends up head down in the barrel, her legs (still chastely covered by her skirt) waving in the air. It all becomes clear: this was the way in which they settled marital disputes in the Middle Ages. If the husband got the wife in the barrel, he'd won the argument. If she clouted him into submission – or unconsciousness – she'd proved her point.

Source: Simon Coupland (with thanks to Rob Parsons).

Bible references: 1 Corinthians 13:4–7; Ephesians 4:26–27,31–32; 5:21–33; Colossians 3:18–19; James 1:19–20; 1 Peter 3:1–9.

59. DATING (Compatibility, Computers, Courtship, Husbands, Marriage, Romance, Singleness, Wives, Humour)

A man who had very specific ideas about what kind of partner he wanted sent in a description to a dating agency. He wrote, 'I want a companion who is small, dark, attractive, loves water sports and enjoys socialising.' The agency put the requirements into their matchmaking computer and it printed out his ideal mate: 'Marry a penguin'.

Source: Adapted from Rob Parsons, Loving Against the Odds (Hodder & Stoughton, 1994), p 213.

Bible references: Genesis 2:18–23; Ruth 3:1–2; Proverbs 18:22; 31:10.

60. EXCUSES (Adultery, Affairs, Commandments, Deception, Husbands, Hypocrisy, Marriage, Sex, Sin, Temptation, Wives)

Jay Lindsay, a Christian counsellor in the United States, has heard Christians attempting to justify their affairs in the most amazing ways. One woman he was seeing said, 'Isn't it wonderful that God has given me two handsome men to love' – meaning her husband and her lover. Another woman told him that God obviously understood and accepted all her affairs because, after all, it was he who had made her this way and given her the need for other men. And to show that it's not just women who come up with excuses like this, one man who was consulting him said about his affair, 'It's OK, because each time we have sex we end up by praying together.'

Source: Adapted from Tom Eisenman, Temptations Men Face (Kingsway, 1991), p 88.

Bible references: Exodus 20:14; Deuteronomy 5:18; Proverbs 6:32–34; Isaiah 5:20–21; Jeremiah 17:9; Matthew 5:27–30; 15:18–20; Mark 7:20–22; Luke 16:15; 2 Timothy 3:1–5; James 2:11.

61. INTIMACY (Books, Hugs, Husbands, Love, Marriage, Men, Wives, Women, Humour)

A woman was browsing in a second-hand bookshop one day when she saw a book that she thought was just what her husband needed to read, so she bought it for him. It was called *How to Hug*. So you can imagine how surprised and delighted she was when that evening she saw him not only leafing through the book, but also reading great chunks of it with obvious interest. It was only then that she discovered her mistake. She had bought him volume 6 of the *Encyclopaedia Britannica*.

Source: Adapted from Sir Godfrey Agnew, in Pass the Port (Christian Brann, 1976), p 11.

Bible references: Song of Songs 2:6; 8:3; 1 Corinthians 13:4–7; Ephesians 5:25–33; Colossians 3:19; 1 Peter 3:7.

62. MEN AND WOMEN (Happiness, Husbands, Love, Lust, Marriage, Sex, Wives, Humour)

Husbands, how to keep your wife happy:
Cherish her, caress her, praise her, pamper her, massage her, fix things for her, empathise with her, serenade her, compliment her, support her, soothe her, humour her, placate her, stroke her, console her, hug her, ignore her fat bits, cuddle her, excite her, pacify her, protect her, phone her, smooch her, nuzzle her, forgive her, entertain her, charm her, carry for her, oblige her, fascinate her, attend to her, trust her, defend her, clothe

her, brag about her, spoil her, embrace her, gratify her, indulge her, idolise her.

Wives, how to keep your husband happy:
Take your clothes off.

Source: Adapted from Allan and Barbara Pease, Why Men Don't Listen and Women Can't Read Maps (Pease Training International, 1999). Used with kind permission of Allan Pease.

Bible references: 1 Corinthians 13:4–7; Ephesians 5:21–33; Colossians 3:18–19; 1 Peter 3:1–9.

63. MISUNDERSTANDING (Communication, Divorce, Husbands, Marriage, Mistakes, Relationships, Wives, Humour)

A farmer once went to see a marriage counsellor and said that his wife wanted a divorce. 'She says our marriage is over,' he said.

'I see,' said the counsellor, 'and does she have good grounds?'

'Oh, aye,' said the farmer, 'about twenty acres which her dad gave her.'

'No, no,' said the counsellor, 'I mean, does she have a good suit?'

'Oh, yes,' replied the farmer. 'Though she mainly keeps it for special occasions.'

'I'm sorry,' said the counsellor, 'What I'm trying to say is, what kind of a case has she got?'

'Oh, right,' said the farmer. 'It's a leather one, not terribly big. I bought it for her a couple of years ago.'

'Look, let's start at the beginning,' said the counsellor with a sigh. 'What exactly is the problem in your marriage?'

'Well,' said the farmer, 'My wife says that I don't understand her, but I can't think why!'

Source: Adapted from Calvin Miller, The Empowered Communicator (Broadman and Holman, 1994), p 31.

Bible references: Matthew 19:3–9; Mark 10:2–12.

64. REMARRIAGE (Divorce, Husbands, Records, Wives, Humour)

The record for the number of times a person has got married was set in January 1997, where else but in Hollywood. The groom was eighty-eight-year-old Scotty Wolfe, a former Baptist pastor, who already held the record for the world's most-married man, with twenty-eight weddings behind him. He married 'middle-aged' Linda Essex, who was herself the record-holder for the world's most-married woman: this was her twenty-third marriage. And for the first time in their lives, this marriage went the distance: Scotty died while the couple were still married.

Source: Simon Coupland.

Bible references: Malachi 2:14–16; Matthew 5:31–32; 19:3–9; Mark 10:2–12; Luke 16:18; Romans 7:2–3; 1 Corinthians 7:10–11.

65. ROMANCE (Husbands, Kissing, Love, Marriage, Newly-weds, Passion, Wives, Humour)

A couple who'd been married for years were saying goodbye one morning as the husband left for work. As usual, he gave his wife a perfunctory peck on the cheek and turned to walk to the car. At that moment, the wife happened to see the husband of the young newly-weds across the road saying goodbye to his wife. He gave her a long passionate kiss, turned to go, then turned back to kiss her again, this time with a long embrace as well. 'Just look at them, dear,' she said. 'Now why don't you ever do that?'

'But darling,' he answered, 'I hardly know the woman!'

Source: Adapted from Haddon Robinson, International Congress of Preachers 1997.

Bible references: Song of Songs 1:2; 5:16.

66. SELFISHNESS (Honeymoon, Husbands, Love, Marriage, Newly-weds, Romance, Service, Wives, Humour)

On the first morning after they'd got back from their honeymoon, the husband went downstairs while his wife was still in bed, and after a while he came back up with breakfast on a tray. 'There,' he said, 'What do you think of that?'

She looked at the tray, which had eggs and bacon, toast and marmalade, orange juice and tea, the post and the paper all beautifully set out, and said, 'It looks fantastic.'

'Great,' he answered. 'That's how I want you to do it for me every morning.'

Source: Adapted from K. Goldstein-Jackson, E. Ford and A.C.H. Newman, The Huge Joke Book (Clarion, 1995), p 114.

Bible references: Romans 12:3; 1 Corinthians 13:1–7; Ephesians 5:25–33; Philippians 2:3–4; Colossians 3:12–14.

67. SEX (Eden, Husbands, Intimacy, Kissing, Marriage, Romance, Wives, Humour)

Adam and Eve had been walking around the garden together for a little while when the Lord realised that they needed a bit of help. So he took Adam on one side and said, 'Adam, when you go for a walk with Eve it would be good to hold her hand.'

'What's a hand?' asked Adam. So God explained it to him.

A little later God said, 'That's good, Adam, but now I think you ought to put your arm round her waist.'

'What's a waist?' asked Adam. So God explained that to him, too.

Another few days passed and the Lord took Adam on one side again, and said, 'Why don't you kiss Eve now?' And of course what Adam wanted to know was, 'What's a kiss?' So God explained.

The next day God sought Adam out again. 'Well done!' he said, 'You're getting along famously. Now go forth and multiply!'

But the next morning Adam was back with another question. 'What's a headache, Lord?'

Source: Adapted from Sir George Middleton in Pass the Port Again (Christian Brann, 1980), p 184.

Bible references: Genesis 1:26–28; 2:18–24; 1 Corinthians 7:3–5.

68. TOLERANCE (Anniversaries, Commitment, Forgiveness, Grudges, Husbands, Love, Marriage, Patience, Sin, Wives, Humour)

A couple were celebrating their golden wedding anniversary, and the wife was asked the secret of their long and happy marriage. She answered, 'On my wedding day, I decided to make a list of ten of my husband's faults which I was always willing to overlook. I reckoned that I could live with ten.'

So someone else asked her which ten faults she had written on her list. 'Well, I never actually did get round to writing them down,' she said. 'So whenever he does something that annoys me, I just say to myself, "It's a good thing for him that that one's on the list!"'

Source: Adapted from The Word for Today, May–July 1998.

Bible references: Proverbs 10:12; 17:9; 1 Corinthians 13:4–5; Ephesians 4:32; Colossians 3:13–14; 1 Thessalonians 5:15; 1 Peter 3:8–9; 4:8.

CHILDREN AND PARENTS

69. CHILDREN (Dinosaurs, Discoveries, Fossils, Geology, Innocence, Parents, Science)

When David Shiffler was three years old, he and his family went on a camping trip to the New Mexico desert west of Albuquerque. He and his dad had just seen the film, *The Land Before Time*, a cartoon adventure in which a group of children get to meet some real dinosaurs, and so David was really keen to hunt for dinosaur eggs. He went digging with a toy trowel and found a green rock which he confidently told his dad was a dinosaur egg. 'Everything he picked up that day was a dinosaur egg,' said his father, who all the same took the rock back home with them and put it in the garage. After David had badgered him about it for two months, Don Shiffler finally gave in and sent the rock off to palaeontologists in Colorado, who told the family that, yes, the rock really was a dinosaur egg. Not only that, it was the oldest meat-eating dinosaur's egg ever found in North America, twice as old as the earliest previously known specimen. In fact, the egg found by three-year-old David convinced scientists that these dinosaurs, called therapods, lived in the Jurassic age, something they hadn't previously suspected.

Source: Adapted from The Times, 20 June 1997.

Bible references: 1 Samuel 3:1–18; 16:1–13; Isaiah 5:21; Matthew 11:25; 18:2–4; 21:14–16; Mark 10:14–16; Luke 10:21; 1 Corinthians 1:17–31.

70. CHURCH (Children, Example, Hypocrisy, Innocence, Intolerance, Joy, Parenting, Patience, Punishment, Smile)

The American writer Erma Bombeck went to church one Sunday and couldn't help noticing a little boy who was looking around and smiling at everyone. He wasn't being naughty or noisy. He wasn't playing around or playing up. He wasn't disturbing anyone else, he was just sitting there smiling. But when his mother noticed, she shook him and said in a loud whisper, 'Stop that grinning! You're in church!' Then she smacked him, and as he started to cry, she said, 'That's better,' and carried on praying.

Source: Adapted from Erma Bombeck, At Wit's End, quoted in Philip Yancey, What's So Amazing about Grace? (Zondervan, 1997), p 32.

Bible references: Ephesians 6:4; Colossians 3:21.

71. FAMILY BREAKDOWN (Anger, Arguments, Children, Conflict, Divorce, Example, Husbands, Marriage, Pain, Parenting, Quarrels, Relationships, Sin, Wives)

We are all too aware that, sadly, married couples can go through stormy times. In one family the husband and wife often ended up having rows, but one particular night the husband just flipped. He pounded the table and stamped on the floor, and shouted at his wife, 'I hate you! I won't take it any more! I've had enough! I won't go on! I won't let it happen! No! No! No!'

Somehow the two of them stayed together, but a few months later the husband was woken up in the middle of the night. He could hear strange noises coming from down the hall where their little boy was sleeping. He went to the room and stood outside the door, and then he heard what the boy was saying. He was only two. But he was repeating word for word what he had heard his parents shouting at each other, 'I hate you! I won't take it any more!... No! No! No!'

In that terrible moment, that man realised just how much of their pain and anger and bitterness he and his wife had passed on to their two-year-old son.

Source: Adapted from Philip Yancey, What's So Amazing about Grace? (Zondervan, 1997), p 120.

Bible references: Jeremiah 31:29–30; Ezekiel 18:1–4; Matthew 5:21–22; Galatians 5:20–21; Ephesians 4:26–27,31–32; Colossians 3:8,21; James 1:19–20.

72. FATHERS (Acceptance, Achievement, Children, Expectations, Failure, God, Parenting, Perfection, School, Self-esteem, Success)

R.T. Kendall is minister of Westminster Chapel and an internationally respected preacher. He has a doctorate in theology from Oxford University and has written a number of books. And yet as a child he felt he could never come up to his father's expectations. No matter how well he did, his father would never be satisfied, he always pushed his son to do better. One day R.T. got A's for all the subjects on his report card except one, and for that he got a B. He cried all the way home because he knew that when he showed it to his father, the one thing his father would comment on was that B. And he was right. His father looked at the card and said, 'Well, pretty good, son. Next time you can have all A's if you really work.'

Similarly, Rob Parsons tells of a middle-aged man he met who was still scarred by the lack of praise and appreciation which his father had given him. One day this man came running home from school to tell his parents that he had got the highest marks in the whole of the county in a music exam. He had scored ninety-seven per cent. He ran into the house and said excitedly, 'Dad, Dad! I came top! I got ninety-seven per cent!' Can you guess what his father answered? 'Won't you ever get full marks?'

Source: Adapted from R.T. Kendall, Ready for God? (Scripture Union, 1995), p 107; Rob Parsons, Loving Against the Odds (Hodder and Stoughton, 1994), p 104.

Bible references: Luke 15:11–32; John 1:12–13; Romans 5:8; 8:31–33; Ephesians 2:4–10; 6:4; Colossians 3:21; 1 John 3:1; 4:8–11.

73. HONESTY (Children, Confession, Families, Lying, Punishment, Sin, Truth, Humour)

Little Johnny is deeply embarrassed by the fact that his house is the last one in the village that still has a privy at the bottom of the garden. He's always being teased about it at school, and so one night he decides to take drastic action. In the early hours, when the house is quiet and everyone's asleep, he creeps down the garden, puts his shoulder to the door of the privy, and with an almighty heave sends it crashing down into the river which runs past the end of their garden.

A little while later his door opens and he knows his parents are looking in at him, but he breathes deeply as if he's sound asleep, and after a while they go away again.

Next morning his father sits him down. 'Now, Johnny,' he says, 'I want you to tell me, did you push the privy into the stream last night?'

'Of course not, Dad!' Johnny says, 'I was fast asleep!'

'Now listen, Johnny,' says Dad, 'I'm going to tell you a story. A long time ago there lived a man named George Washington. One day he chopped down his father's cherry tree. And when his father asked him whether he'd done it, he said, "Father, I cannot tell a lie. I did." And his father was pleased that he'd told the truth, and so he didn't punish him. Now let me ask you again, did you or did you not push the privy into the stream last night?'

'All right, Dad,' says Johnny, 'I cannot tell a lie. I did.'

So his father grabs him by the scruff of the neck and puts him across his knee, and starts to smack his bottom. 'But, Dad,' sobs Johnny, 'You told me that George Washington's daddy didn't punish him because he told the truth.'

'Aye,' says his dad. 'But George Washington's father wasn't in the cherry tree at the time!'

Source: Adapted from Jonathan Wilmot, Paris, 1981.

Bible references: Leviticus 19:11; Proverbs 6:16–19; 12:22; Zechariah 8:16; Ephesians 4:25; Colossians 3:9.

74. LOVE (Atonement, Brothers, Christ, Death, Families, Sacrifice, Sickness, Suffering)

An eight-year-old boy had a younger sister who was dying of leukaemia. His parents explained that if the little girl didn't have a blood transfusion she would die, and asked her brother whether he would be willing to be tested to see whether his blood was compatible with hers. He said that was OK, and when the blood was tested, it proved to be a perfect match. Then they asked if he would be willing to give her a pint of his blood, as it was her only hope. He said he would need to think about that one overnight.

Next day the boy said that he had thought it over, and that he was happy to give his sister the blood that she needed. They took him to hospital and put him on a stretcher next to his sister. The nurse took a pint of the boy's blood, and it was given to his sister. The boy lay there quietly while the transfusion was being given, until a doctor came over to ask how he was doing. Then he asked the doctor, 'How soon is it until I start to die?'

Source: Adapted from Anna Lamott, no reference given, in John Ortberg, Love Beyond Reason (Zondervan, 1998), pp 24–25.

Bible references: Isaiah 53:4–7; Matthew 20:28; 26:26–28; Mark 10:45; 14:22–24; Luke 22:19–20; John 1:29,36; 3:14–17; Romans 4:25; 5:6–11; 8:1–4; 1 Corinthians 5:7; 15:3; 2 Corinthians 5:14–15; 1 Thessalonians 5:10; 1 Timothy 2:5–6; Titus 2:14; Hebrews 9:15,28; 1 Peter 1:18–19; 2:24–25; 3:18; 1 John 3:16.

75. MISTAKES (Baptism, Birth, Children, Clergy, Gender, History, Names, Parents, Humour)

On 21 December 1818 the vicar of St Nicholas' church in Great Yarmouth baptised a baby named Susannah. Nothing unusual in that. But the baptismal register has a note added later which reads, 'Rebaptized 5 Jany 1819, when the names given were Richard Drury'!

Source: Adapted from Don Lewis, Reverend Sirs, Ladies and Gentlemen (Mowbrays, 1971), p 52.

76. NAMES (Bible, Children, Discipleship, History, Old Testament, Puritans, Humour)

In the seventeenth century a number of Puritans delighted in calling their children by long, morally uplifting names. I mentioned some of these in *A Dose of Salts* (story 194); others which parents in the American colonies gave their children included Small-Hope, Fear-Not, The-Lord-Is-Near, Be-Courteous, and Kill-Sin. Somewhat more exotic, if not downright cryptic, were Job-Raked-Out-of-the-Ashes and Misericordia-Adulterina.

Other parents took their children's names directly from the Bible. This led to unfortunate seventeenth-century Puritan children in America being called Mahershalalhashbaz (after the son of the prophet Isaiah), Zaphnathpaaneah (which was the name Pharaoh gave to Joseph), and Mene Mene Tekel Upharsin (the message written on the wall at Belshazzar's feast).

Others apparently asked God to show them what to call their newborn children by closing their eyes, opening the Bible at random and putting their finger on a word. That at least is thought to be the explanation of such unusual names as Maybe Barnes and Notwithstanding Griswold.

Source: Adapted from Bill Bryson, Made in America (Minerva, 1995), p 140.

Bible references: Genesis 17:5,15; 25:25–26; 29:32 – 30:24; 35:10; 41:45; Judges 6:32; Ruth 1:20; Job 2:8; Isaiah 7:3,14; 8:1; Jeremiah 20:3; Daniel 5:25–28; Hosea 1:4–9; Matthew 1:21,23.

77. NAMES (Baptism, Children, Law, Parents, Humour)

In 1997 the Swedish authorities refused to grant a couple permission to register their son's name as Brfxxccxxmnpckccccllllmmnprxvclmnckssqlbbllll6 (pronounced Albin!). Instead they were fined £390 and told to find a shorter name. So they did, and called the child 'A'. Unfortunately the authorities replied that single letter names were also prohibited.

Source: Adapted from The Times, 4 September 1997.

78. RECONCILIATION (Children, Estrangement, Families, Fathers, Forgiveness, Love, Parents, Relationships, Sons)

Ernest Hemingway once wrote a short story set in Spain, in which a father and son fell out with one another. The boy ran away to Madrid, so the father disowned him in disgust, and said he didn't want anything more to do with him. Years later, the father realised that he'd been too harsh, and how much he missed his son. He wanted to put things right and to see his boy again. So he put an advert in a Madrid newspaper, 'Paco, meet me at the Hotel Montana at noon on Tuesday. All is forgiven. Papa.' But Paco is a common name in Spain, and when the father turned up at the hotel at noon on Tuesday, hoping that his son would be there, he had to force his way through the crowd of young men waiting outside the hotel, all named Paco, and all longing to be reconciled with their fathers.

Source: Adapted from Philip Yancey, True Confessions (Word, 1987), pp 42–43.

Bible references: Genesis 46:29; Malachi 4:6; Luke 1:17; 15:11–32; John 1:12–13; Romans 5:8–11; 8:31–33; 2 Corinthians 5:17–20; Ephesians 6:4; Colossians 3:21; 1 John 3:1; 4:8–11.

79. RESURRECTION (Children, Church, Crucifix, Death, Easter, Jesus, Misunderstanding, Humour)

The parish church next to Arundel Castle is full of impressive tombs and monuments, including, on the wall facing the door, a large crucifix. One day a girl of about nine or ten walked in and saw this, then turned to her parents and said, 'Oh, so is this where Jesus is buried?'

Source: Simon Coupland.

Bible references: Matthew 28:1–10; Mark 16:1–8; Luke 24:1–43; John 20:1–31; Acts 1:1–3; 2:24,32; 13:30–37; 17:31–32; Romans 1:3–4; 1 Corinthians 15:1–8,12–20; 1 Peter 1:21.

80. SELF-ESTEEM (Adolescence, Children, Confidence, Families, Love, Parents, Rebellion, Relationships, Sex, Teenagers)

Michael Parkinson once asked Dawn French during an interview what had given her her self-esteem and confidence in herself. She replied:

I've tried to wonder what it was that gave me confidence from early on, and I can only put it down to my dad. I remember that there was a night when I was going to go out to a disco, and I was really ready to do sex with anybody who wanted to ask me. I had some purple suede hot pants that I thought I looked great in. And my father called me into his office and sat me down, and I thought, 'I'm going to get the lecture, blah blah.' And instead of giving me a lecture about what time to be home or any of that he just said to me, 'You are the most precious thing in our lives and you are beautiful, and you are worthy of anybody who shows you any attention. You shouldn't feel grateful for the scraps that any other girls leave behind: you should have the best.'

And I went out, and in fact no boy came within ten yards of me! I wouldn't allow them because they were beneath me. He just gave me a bit of self-esteem.

Source: Parkinson, BBC TV, 8 January 1999.

Bible references: Ephesians 6:4; Colossians 3:21.

81. TODDLERS (Children, Human nature, Ownership, Possessions, Selfishness, Humour)

Property law from a toddler's perspective:

If I like it, it's mine.
If I can take it away from you, it's mine.
If I had it a while ago, it's mine.
If I say it is mine, it's mine.
If it looks like mine, it's mine.
If I say I saw it first, it's mine.

If you're having fun with it, it's mine.
If you put down your toy, it's mine.
If it's broken, it's yours.

Source: Joke Distribution Network (joke.network@juno.com), quoted in Leadership Journal, Spring 1998.

82. WITNESS (Air travel, Children, Disability, Embarrassment, Evangelism, Flying, the Gospel, Salvation, Self-consciousness)

A man was once flying from Atlanta to Dallas, and it so happened that in the seat next to him there was a little girl with Down's syndrome. After a while she turned to him and said, 'Do you smoke?' 'No,' he said, 'I don't smoke.'

'That's good,' she said, 'My mummy says you shouldn't smoke.' Then she pointed to the businessman who was sitting the other side of him and said, 'Does he smoke?'

The man was naturally rather embarrassed by this, but he thought he ought to humour her, so he asked the businessman sitting next to him, 'Excuse me, but do you smoke?' 'No,' he said. 'That's good,' said the girl.

There was a bit of a pause, and then a few minutes later the little girl said, 'Do you love Jesus?'

'Yes,' the man replied, 'As a matter of fact I do love Jesus.'

'That's good,' she said. 'Everyone should love Jesus.' And then it suddenly dawned on him what she was going to say next. And he hunched down in his seat and hoped against hope that she wouldn't. But she did. 'That man next to you,' she said, 'does he love Jesus?'

So he swallowed hard, and turned to the businessman sitting next to him, and asked him.

And with a tear in his eye the man replied, 'Do you know, I've been wanting someone to ask me that for a long time.'

And so Milton Cunningham, who was a preacher on his way to speak at a seminary in Dallas, led that businessman to Christ there on that aeroplane, all thanks to a little girl's utter lack of self-consciousness.

Source: Adapted from Jim Rea, International Congress of Preachers 1997.

Bible references: Matthew 10:32–33; 11:25; 18:2–4; 21:14–16; Mark 8:38; 10:14–16; Luke 9:26; 10:21; 12:8–9; Romans 1:16–17; 2 Timothy 1:8; 1 John 2:23.

SUFFERING AND DEATH

83. BLAME (Answered prayer, Courage, Cruelty, Evil, Faith, Free will, God, Hardship, Holocaust, Human nature, Jews, Mercy, Murder, Nazism, Sacrifice, Second World War, Suffering, Voice of God, War, Why?)

Irene Opdyke lives in America now, but she was born and brought up in pre-war Poland. Like so many of her generation, during the war she witnessed appalling brutality and terrible suffering. The worst moment came when she was working in a German army kitchen in the town of Lvov. The persecution of the Jews was at its height. She saw them being brought in lorries, being herded into the town square, being shot: men, women and, worst of all, children, even babies pulled from their mothers' arms. As a Christian, the thought went through her mind: 'God, where are you? Where are you? Why are you not doing something?' Looking back, fifty years later, she said, 'I couldn't understand that. I said, "God, you're a figment of my imagination!" I remember, I cried and I prayed and finally I fell asleep, and when I came to there was a feeling in my heart. Not with the words, but God said, "This is people's fault." God gave us free will to choose what we want to be, what road we take, the evil one or the good one. It's up to us. The answer was so powerful that I asked God for forgiveness and I asked him for help. And now I said, even if my life depends, please help me to help. And God did this.'

She went on to save the lives of twelve Jews. She did it by hiding them in the cellar of the house where she was working, which was, incredibly, the home of a German officer. Thanks to her, all twelve survived the war. Irene not only saw that it was people who were responsible for this terrible crime. She also realised that she could do something about it, and she did.

Source: Adapted from The Telegraph magazine, 15 May 1999.

Bible references: Deuteronomy 30; Joshua 24:15; 1 Kings 18:21; Psalms 14:2–3; 42:3; 74; 79; 80:1–7; 115:2; Isaiah 63:15 – 64:2; Malachi 2:17; 3:13–18; Matthew 7:13–14.

84. DEPRESSION (Afterlife, Death, Despair, Fear, Honesty, Prayer, Sickness, Suffering, Suicide)

A committed Christian suffering from depression wrote the following prayer:

> Dear Jesus
>
> Really the trouble is that we don't want to be here at all. This big black cloud that we don't like and don't really understand looms over our lives and shuts out the sun. We want to run away – best of all to run away and be with you. We want to scream and scream and scream all the madness and the badness out, but we're afraid of people hearing and so we lock it all up inside.
>
> Why do you want us here? What do you want to do with us? We really don't think we can cope –

> neither with the present nor with the future. We're afraid of the dark, Lord; please help us. Please. Often when we wake up in the morning we wish we hadn't. We wish the day didn't exist, and we could just slip into oblivion. Not night, because often that's filled with nasty dreams. But nice, quiet, peaceful oblivion. Best of all, with you.

Source: Quoted with permission.

Bible references: 1 Kings 19:3–4; Job 3:20–26; 7:11–16; Psalms 42; 43; 88; 143; Jeremiah 20:14–18; Jonah 4:1–8; 2 Corinthians 5:1–4; Philippians 1:21–24.

85. DESPAIR (Afterlife, Comedy, Death, Depression, Epitaphs, Failure, Fame, Remembrance, Success, Suicide, Humour)

Tony Hancock, the great British comedian, died of an overdose in 1968. His last TV monologue, recorded four years earlier, contained this desperately sad reflection on life:

> What have you achieved? What have you achieved? You lost your chance, me old son. You contributed absolutely nothing to this life. A waste of time you being here at all. No place for you in Westminster Abbey. The best you can expect is a few daffodils in a jam jar, a rough hewn stone bearing the legend, 'He came and he went, and in between – nothing!' Nobody will even notice you're not here. After about a year afterwards somebody might say down the pub, 'Where's old Hancock? I haven't seen him around lately.' 'Oh, he's dead you know.' 'Oh, is he?' A right raison d'être that is. Nobody will ever know I existed. Nothing to leave behind me. Nothing to

> pass on. Nobody to mourn me. That's the bitterest blow of all.

Source: Quoted in Jonathon Green, Famous Last Words (Chancellor Press, 1993).

Bible references: Job 7:6–10; 14:1–2; Psalms 39:4–6; 49; 90:3–12; 103:15–16; 144:3–4; Ecclesiastes 1:2–11; 2:15–16; 12:6–8; Isaiah 40:7–8.

86. FAITH (Afterlife, Assurance, Death, Forgiveness, God, Grief, Grudges, Heaven, Loss, Mourning, Suffering, Terrorism, Violence, Witness)

On Remembrance Day in 1987 the Northern Irish town of Enniskillen was torn apart by an IRA bomb. Eleven people were killed and many more injured. Among those who died was a twenty-year-old nurse, Marie Wilson, home for the weekend from Belfast's Victoria Hospital. Among the injured was her father Gordon. His words that evening echoed round the world:

> I bear no ill will. I bear no grudge. Dirty sort of talk is not going to bring her back to life. She was a great wee lassie. She loved her profession. She was a pet and she is dead. She is in heaven, and we will meet again.
>
> Don't ask me please for a purpose. I don't have a purpose. I don't have an answer. But I know that there has to be a plan. If I didn't think that, I would commit suicide. It is part of a greater plan and God is good. And we shall meet again.

Source: Adapted from the Church of England Newspaper.

Bible references: Genesis 22:1–14; Isaiah 55:9–11; Jeremiah 10:23; Matthew 5:38–48; Luke 6:27–36; 23:34; Acts 7:60; 8:1; Romans 8:28; 12:14,17–21; 1 Corinthians 1:17–31; 2 Corinthians 1:8–11; 4:7–12; Ephesians 4:32; Colossians 3:13; 1 Thessalonians 5:15; 1 Peter 3:8–9.

87. FREEDOM (the Cross, Death, Decisions, Discipleship, Endurance, Evil, Free will, Hardship, Holocaust, Hope, Human nature, Nazism, Sacrifice, Second World War, Suffering)

Victor Frankl spent three years in four different concentration camps, including Auschwitz. His suffering was appalling. But his spirit was never broken. After the war he wrote his reflections on the experience of camp life:

> We who lived in concentration camps can remember the men who walked through the huts comforting others, giving away their last piece of bread. They may have been few in number, but they offer sufficient proof that everything can be taken from a man but one thing: the last of the human freedoms – to choose one's attitude in any given set of circumstances, to choose one's own way.
>
> And there are always choices to make. Every day, every hour, offered the opportunity to make a decision, a decision which determined whether you would or would not submit to those powers which threatened to rob you of your very self, your inner freedom; which determined whether or not you would become the plaything of circumstance, renouncing freedom and dignity to become moulded into the form of the typical inmate....
>
> Even though conditions such as lack of sleep,

insufficient food and various mental stresses may suggest that the inmates were bound to react in certain ways, in the final analysis it becomes clear that the sort of person the prisoner became was the result of an inner decision, and not the result of camp influences alone. Fundamentally therefore, any man can, even under such circumstances, decide what shall become of him – mentally and spiritually.... It is this spiritual freedom – which cannot be taken away – that makes life meaningful and purposeful....

If there is a meaning in life at all, then there must be a meaning in suffering. Suffering is an ineradicable part of life, even as fate and death. Without suffering and death human life cannot be complete. The way a man accepts his fate and all the suffering it entails, the way in which he takes up his cross, gives him ample opportunity – even under the most difficult circumstances – to add a deeper meaning to his life.

Source: Victor Frankl, Man's Search for Meaning (Hodder and Stoughton, 1987), pp 65-67. © 1962 by Victor Frankl. Reproduced by kind permission of Hodder and Stoughton Limited.

Bible references: Job 36:21; Matthew 10:37–39; 16:24–26; Mark 8:34–37; Luke 9:23–25; 14:27; Acts 20:22–24; Romans 5:3; 8:17–18,35–39; 2 Corinthians 4:7 – 5:9; Colossians 1:24; 2 Timothy 1:8–12; Hebrews 11:25–26; 1 Peter 1:6–9; 4:19.

88. HEALING (Afterlife, Cancer, Church, Death, Faith, Fear, God, Heaven, Sickness, Suffering, Televangelists, Theology)

Gordon Fee, the New Testament theologian, contrasts two true stories.

Stan was in his mid-twenties, married, a vital member of our local church, but he lay dying from a large tumour on his spine. I went to visit him with fear and trepidation. I was scarcely twenty, knew little about death and dying, and certainly knew that I was too young to be of much comfort. But I went because he was also my friend, and I am a Pentecostal, who believes that God heals the sick.

I have never forgotten my experience that day, for what happened to me happened to all who visited him. We went with due apprehension, not knowing what to say; but Stan's own experience of Christ's presence, what he was learning about God's love, and his readiness – dare I say a kind of Pauline eagerness – to be with his Lord was so infectious that we all left Stan's presence built up in our God. We went to comfort him; we left having been ministered to by him. He died three months later, a Pentecostal who also trusted to the very end that God might show him mercy through healing; but he died without disillusionment, because he was ready to enter his eternal reward.

The second story happened many years later, on a Sunday morning, when our eldest son was in front of the TV. There on the screen was the wife of one of the then well-known televangelists. She was pointing her finger at the television audience with a brittle harshness. 'If any of you out there are dying of cancer,' she nearly shouted, 'it's your fault, not God's. God wants to heal you.'

Two stories; two followers of Christ. I prefer the former.

Source: Gordon Fee, Paul, the Spirit and the People of God (Hendrickson, 1996), pp 140–141. Reproduced by kind permission of Hendrickson Publishers, Inc.

Bible references: Acts 20:22–24; Romans 5:3; 8:18,35–39; 2 Corinthians 4:16 – 5:9; Philippians 1:21–24; 2:25–30; 1 Timothy 5:23; 2 Timothy 1:12; 4:6–8; James 5:14–16; 1 Peter 1:6–9; 4:19.

89. HEAVEN (Afterlife, Death, Diet, Food, Health, Lifestyle, Old age, Humour)

An elderly couple were well known in their church for their healthy lifestyle. The wife made sure that their diet was carefully controlled – low in sugar, low in salt, low in fat; high in fibre, high in fruit, high in fish – even though her husband was known to be none too keen on all this. Faddishness he called it, but every time he grumbled, she pointed out to him what good health they enjoyed at what was, he had to admit, a ripe old age.

Eventually the husband died, and not long afterwards his wife followed him. When she arrived at the pearly gates, he was there to welcome her, and he gave her a tour of heaven. At every turn he pointed out how wonderful it all was, how beautiful everything was, in fact, how much better it was in every way to life on earth. And she couldn't help but agree. So in the end he couldn't contain himself any longer. 'Just think,' he burst out, 'how much sooner we could have enjoyed all this if we hadn't followed all your silly fads!'

Source: Adapted from Phil Mason, ed., Christian Crackers 9 (Norheimsund Books, 1993).

Bible references: Romans 8:18,35–39; 2 Corinthians 4:16 – 5:9; Philippians 1:21–24; 2 Peter 3:13; Revelation 21:1–5.

90. JUSTICE (Afterlife, Death, Dictators, Fear, Judgement, Peace, Retribution, Suffering)

It seems terribly wrong that while millions of Stalin's victims died before their time, many of them in agony, the Soviet dictator should have died peacefully in his bed at the age of seventy-three. And yet his last hours were in fact far from peaceful. He was afraid that his comrades were trying to supplant him, suspicious of Zionist and Titoist conspiracies, and troubled by rumours that Jewish doctors were poisoning the country's leaders, including himself.

His daughter Svetlana described his last moments: 'God grants an easy death only to the just. At what seemed like the very last moment, he cast a glance over everyone in the room, a terrible glance, perhaps angry and full of fear of death.... He suddenly lifted his left hand as though he were bringing down a curse on us all.' Then he died.

Source: Adapted from The Daily Telegraph, 30 May 1998.

Bible references: Genesis 18:25; Deuteronomy 32:4; Job 21:7–15; Psalms 73; 82; Ecclesiastes 3:16–17; 4:1; Jeremiah 12:1–4; Matthew 16:27; 25:31–46; John 5:26–29; Acts 17:31; Romans 2:5–11; 2 Corinthians 5:10; 2 Thessalonians 1:6–10; Hebrews 9:27; Revelation 20:11–15.

91. LAST WORDS (Afterlife, Arrogance, Atheism, Death, Despair, Forgiveness, God, Guilt, Heaven, Hell, Humility, Hymns, Judgement, Life, Modesty, Ownership, Possessions, Power, Pride, Repentance, Retribution, Royalty, Science, Sin, Time, Unbelief, Wealth, Humour)

- Queen Elizabeth I, died 1603: 'All my possessions for one moment of time!'
- Dominique Bouhours, French grammarian, died 1702: 'I am about to, or I am going to, die. Either expression is used.'
- Aurungzebe, Emperor of Hindustan, died 1707: 'What is the use? Every torture that I have inflicted, every sin that I have committed, every wrong that I have done, I carry the consequences with me. Strange that I came with nothing into the world and now go away with this stupendous caravan of sin; wherever I look I see only God. I have greatly sinned and I know not what torment awaits me.'
- Sir Isaac Newton, died 1727: 'I don't know what I may seem to the world. But as to myself, I seem to have been only a boy playing on the seashore and diverting myself in now and then finding a smoother pebble or prettier shell than the ordinary, whilst the great ocean of truth lay all undiscovered before me.'
- Matthew Tindall, militant atheist, died 1733: 'Oh God, if there be a God, I desire thee to have mercy on me!'
- Heinrich Heine, German poet, died 1856. Told on his deathbed: 'Dieu vous pardonnera' ('God will forgive you'). He replied, 'Oui, c'est son métier' ('Yes, that's his job').

- Prince Albert, died 1861: 'I have had wealth, rank and power, but if these were all, how wretched I should be. Rock of ages, cleft for me, let me hide myself in thee.'
- Lord Palmerston, British Prime Minister, died 1865: 'Die, my dear doctor? That's the last thing I shall do!'

Source: Quoted in Jonathon Green, Famous Last Words (Chancellor Press, 1993).

Bible references: Job 1:21; Isaiah 28:14–15; Amos 9:10; Matthew 10:28,32–33; 16:24–27; Mark 8:36–38; Luke 9:25–26; 12:4–5,16–21; 16:19–31; Acts 26:18; 2 Corinthians 4:4; Hebrews 9:27.

92. MOURNING (Afterlife, Assurance, Death, Depression, Evangelicals, Faith, Grief, Heaven, History, Holiness, Judgement, Secularism, Unbelief, Victorians)

To people today the Victorians can seem excessively morbid. Paintings of deathbed scenes, the rituals of mourning, and the long, many would say excessive, grief of Queen Victoria all conjure up an image of a society which had an unhealthy preoccupation with death. But a scholarly study of *Death in the Victorian Family* shows that most people came through bereavement positively and decisively as a result of their strong evangelical faith. The Queen was a rare exception. As one reviewer of the book, herself no fan of evangelicalism, commented, 'Death had no sting for people who lived in constant readiness for the moment when they would be "called away". Judgement held no horrors for those who had been trying for a moral life as long as they could remember.'

The book also shows that it was the increasing unbelief of the later part of the century which led to people having difficulty facing death. For example, Charles Darwin couldn't cope with a string of family bereavements, but withdrew more and more into himself and eventually ended up severely depressed. For instance, when his cousin's wife died, Darwin wrote a letter of condolence, as was expected. But he had little comfort to offer except the fact that her suffering was over. This is such a contrast to the heart-felt and positive sympathy offered by Gladstone in similar circumstances, based on his strong Christian faith and his firm belief in life after death.

What this book shows is that evangelical faith offered a powerful means of facing death with realism and confidence, much of which was lost when the nation became increasingly secular as the century went on.

Source: Adapted from a review by Kathryn Hughes of Pat Jalland, Death in the Victorian Family in The Daily Telegraph, 2 November 1996.

Bible references: Job 19:25–26; Isaiah 26:19; Hosea 13:14; Matthew 5:4; John 5:28–29; 6:39–40; 11:25–26; Romans 6:4–8; 8:11; 1 Corinthians 6:14; 15:12–57; Philippians 3:20–21; 1 Thessalonians 4:13–18.

93. PAIN (Cancer, Claustrophobia, the Cross, Fear, Hardship, Healing, Jesus, Prayer, Presence of God, Rape, Sickness, Suffering)

The preacher, writer and church leader John Wimber, who died in 1997, was well known for his witness to a God who works miracles. But before his death he spoke at Holy Trinity, Brompton about suffering, based on the experience of his own treatment for cancer.

A question that has often been asked me is, 'Did you commune with the Lord through this time?' Commune with the Lord? I was unconscious. I slept twenty to twenty-two hours a day. They had to carry me out of the bed to go get the treatment. They put you under this thing and they clamp this other thing over your head.

I found out that I was claustrophobic. They take straps and they put them over you. You have to be totally immobilised for this treatment because radiation is an exact art, and if they miss they could fry your brain in a few seconds. I was absolutely frightened out of my wits for all forty-three treatments.

But the Lord was there in the midst of the fear, in the midst of the panic, in the midst of the horror. He was always there.

Some years ago, I counselled a woman who had been brutally raped. She had been through extensive counselling. She was a Christian and told me how at the time of the rape, she had been crying out, 'Jesus, Jesus, Jesus... '

She asked me, 'Where was Jesus?'

I felt the Lord gave me the answer. I told her, 'He was being raped.'

Source: UK Focus, December 1997. Reproduced by kind permission of Holy Trinity, Brompton.

Bible references: Acts 9:4–5; Romans 8:17; 2 Corinthians 1:3–11; 4:7–12; Philippians 3:10–11; Colossians 1:24; 1 Peter 4:12–13.

94. SEARCHING (Change, Children, Death, Evil, Faith, God, Grief, Hope, Prayer, Religion, Repentance, Spirituality, Suffering, Violence, Youth)

The small Scottish town of Dunblane became known across the world in March 1996 when a gunman walked into a primary school and shot dead sixteen children and their teacher. John Drane, a clergyman and writer, visited the town shortly after the massacre.

> I made my way to the school gates, which had become a centre of devotion, transformed by the flowers and other offerings placed there by local people and strangers alike. The street was deserted apart from a handful of police officers and a gang of youths aged about seventeen to twenty. As I watched, they took from their pockets sixteen night-light candles – one for each dead child – and, kneeling on the damp pavement, arranged them in a circle and lit them using glowing cigarettes.
>
> They stood around the candles for a moment, then one of them broke the silence. 'I suppose somebody should say something.' As they wondered how to do it, one of them spotted me, identified me as a minister and called me over with the words, 'You will know what to say.'
>
> The reality was quite different. As I stood there, tears streaming down my face, I had no idea what to say or how to say it. So we stood, holding on to one another for a moment; then I said a brief prayer.
>
> That was the catalyst that enabled them to start praying. A question came first: 'What kind of world is this?' Another asked, 'Is there any hope?' Someone said, 'I wish I could trust God.' 'I'll need to change,' said a fourth one, glancing over his shoul-

der at the police who were on duty. He reached into his pocket, and I saw that he had a knife. He knelt again by the ring of candles and quietly said, 'I'll not be needing this now,' as he tucked the weapon under some of the flowers lying nearby. One of the other youths produced what looked like a piece of bicycle chain and did the same. We stood silently for a moment; then we went our separate ways.

Source: National Bible Society of Scotland, quoted in Word in Action 97, issue 82. Reproduced by kind permission of the Bible Society.

Bible references: Ecclesiastes 3:11; Acts 14:15–17; 17:22–31; Romans 1:19–20; 2:14–15.

95. SUFFERING (Christianity, the Cross, Faith, God, Jesus, Meaning, Modern life)

The poet R.S. Thomas said in a BBC interview: 'I am a Christian because I think Christianity is the most profound and satisfactory answer to the great problem of suffering. I don't think even in this late stage of the twentieth century there is anything more contemporary than the cross. I would not be content to find an answer to the problem of suffering which didn't involve God.'

Source: Quoted by Richard Harries in The Times, 23 December 1995.

Bible references: Psalm 22; Isaiah 53; Matthew 20:18–19,28; 26:2; 27:32–50; Mark 10:45; 15:21–37; Luke 24:26–46; John 3:14–17; 19:16–37; Romans 4:25; 5:6–11; 8:1–4; 1 Corinthians 1:18–24; 2:2; 15:3; 2 Corinthians 5:14–15; Galatians 3:13; 6:14; Philippians 2:6–8; 1 Thessalonians 5:10; 1 Timothy 2:5–6; Titus 2:14; Hebrews 9:15,28; 12:2; 1 Peter 1:18–19; 2:21–24; 3:18.

96. WHY? (Accidents, Air travel, Death, Flying, God, Grief, Meaning, Pain, Suffering)

Some years ago a young American called Glenn Chambers was flying from New York to Quito in Ecuador on what was, for him, the trip of a lifetime. He was going to fulfil his dream of working in a radio station, the Voice of the Andes. But as the plane was flying over Colombia, the pilots failed to see a mountain looming up ahead of them, and by the time they did, it was too late to take evasive action. The aircraft smashed into the mountainside, burning wreckage tumbled down into the valley far below, and Glenn Chambers, like the other passengers, never had a chance. There were no survivors.

A little while later Glenn's mother got a note through the post. It was the last thing that her son had ever written. It was a page from a magazine that he'd picked up from the floor of the airport, just an advert which had plenty of white space to write on, because it only had one word printed on it. The one word was 'Why?' And as Glenn Chambers' mother read and reread her son's last words, that single word, 'Why?' screamed up at her from the paper.

Source: Adapted from Charles Swindoll, For Those Who Hurt, quoted in Haddon Robinson, Biblical Preaching (IVP, 1986), pp 162–163.

Bible references: Genesis 18:25; Job 1 – 2; Isaiah 45:7; Lamentations 3:38–40; James 5:10–11.

LEAVING GOD OUT OF IT

97. COMPROMISE (Church, Clergy, Holocaust, Hypocrisy, Jews, Nazism, Second World War, Suffering)

Steve Chalke tells of the time when he was making a television programme about forgiveness. For part of it he went over to Auschwitz in Poland, the site of one of the most terrible concentration camps of the Second World War, and while he was there he met an old man who had lived in that area during the war. The man described how the railway tracks leading to Auschwitz passed through his village, and as the trains loaded with Jews went past the houses, the men, women and children crammed into the cattle trucks would scream at the tops of their voices to draw attention to themselves, in the hopes of making someone hear. And he described how on Sundays, when he was in church with the other villagers, as they heard the rattle of the carriages in the distance, coming nearer, the minister would tell them all to sing louder. To drown the screams of the victims passing by, he would urge the congregation, 'Sing, sing, sing!'

Source: Adapted from Steve Chalke, Worthing 1999.

Bible references: 1 Samuel 15:22; Psalm 51:16–17; Proverbs 21:3; Isaiah 1:11–17; Jeremiah 7:21–26; Hosea 6:6; Amos 5:21–24; Micah 6:6–8; Matthew 23:23–24; Luke 11:42.

98. COUNTERFEIT RELIGION (Christ, Communism, Dictators, False prophets, Holy communion, Intercession, Jesus, Prayer, Unlikely Messiahs)

In its edition of 17 February 1950, the Communist newspaper *Pravda* wrote, wittingly or otherwise, a parody of prayer:

> If you meet with difficulties in your work, or suddenly doubt your abilities, think of him – of Stalin – and you will find the confidence you need. If you feel tired in an hour when you should not, think of him – of Stalin – and your work will go well. If you are seeking a correct decision, think of him – of Stalin – and you will find that decision.

And in another conscious or unconscious echo of Christianity, during the Communist era the Soviet authorities put up signs all around Russia which read: 'Lenin Lived. Lenin Lives. Lenin Will Live.'

Source: Quoted in Philip Yancey, Praying with the KGB (Multnomah, 1992), pp 69, 79.

Bible references: Isaiah 14:13–14; Ezekiel 28:2; Daniel 6:6–9; 11:36–37; Acts 12:21–23; 2 Thessalonians 2:4; Revelation 13:4–5.

99. CRUELTY (Animals, Compassion, Creation, Dogs, God, Human nature, Social action)

The story is told that Robert Louis Stevenson was once out walking in an Edinburgh street when he came across a man beating his dog. Stevenson was horrified; he grabbed hold of the man by the lapels and pushed him against the wall, telling him to stop. The man told him to mind his own business, 'It's my dog and I'll do what I want with it.' 'It's not your dog,' replied Stevenson, 'It's God's dog, and I'm here to protect it.'

Source: Adapted from Eugene H. Peterson, Where Your Treasure Is (Eerdmans, 1993), p 139.

Bible references: Genesis 1:24–26; 2:19; 9:2; Psalms 8:6–8; 24:1; 50:10–12; 104:24–30; Jeremiah 27:5.

100. DEATH (Afterlife, Computers, Human nature, Immortality, the Internet, Modern life, Reputation, Humour)

The Viking poem Hávamál ('The Sayings of the High One') put it bluntly: 'Cattle die, kinsmen die, all men must die; I know of just one thing which never dies: the reputation a person leaves behind.' A thousand years later, it's still one way in which people think they can live on after their death, as a report in the *San José Mercury News* shows. People in California are trying to achieve immortality by putting a web address on their gravestones. The idea is that loved ones or even curious strangers can log on to a website which commemorates the life and times of the deceased in pictures, words, music and video clips. Cemeteries in San José and Hollywood ('the Forever Cemetery') say that they want to 'fill in the dash between the date of birth and the date of death with a dot com', as one cemetery owner put it.

Source: Adapted from The Times, 29 November 1999.

Bible references: Job 7:6–10; 14:1–2,5; Psalms 39:4–6; 49; 90:3–12; 103:15–16; 144:3–4; Ecclesiastes 1:11; 2:15–16; Isaiah 40:7–8.

101. THE DEVIL (Advertising, Afterlife, Death, Heaven, Hell, Marketing, Humour)

A man dies and finds himself standing at the pearly gates. St Peter comes out to greet him, but looks a bit puzzled. 'We weren't expecting anyone just now,' he says, 'just wait here a minute while I look up your records on the computer.' The man stands there, and waits, and waits, and while he's waiting he notices a wild party going on down among the clouds. There's music and laughter, food and dancing, and the people are obviously having a great time. 'I wonder where that is?' he thinks to himself. 'It's obviously not heaven, but it looks far too much fun to be hell.' At that moment the gate opens again, and St Peter comes out scratching his head. 'I'm really sorry to keep you,' he says, 'but we can't find your records at all. If you wouldn't mind waiting a bit longer, I'll go and have another look.' So the man stands there twiddling his thumbs, and every so often looking down at the cloud where the party's still in full swing. He waits and waits, and eventually he makes up his mind, and jumps down to join the party. But he falls straight through the cloud and lands slap bang in front of the devil. It's boiling hot, the flames are shooting up around him, and the devil grins at him and says, 'Welcome to hell!' 'But I didn't want to come here,' the man stammers, 'I just wanted to join the party.' 'Ah,' the devil replies, 'I see you've come across our marketing department.'

Source: Adapted from Robin Marsland, Worthing 1998.

Bible references: Genesis 3:1–5; Matthew 4:1–11; Luke 4:1–13; 2 Corinthians 2:11; 11:14.

102. EVIL (Belief, Demons, the Devil, Dogs, Exorcism, Human nature, Satanism, Scepticism)

How do we account for evil? Is it only in people's hearts, or is there a force of evil 'out there', something – or someone – outside of human beings? When David Hay of Nottingham University questioned a representative sample of people in the general public about their religious experience, one interesting, and perhaps surprising, feature that emerged was that no fewer than 12% had at some time or other had an 'awareness of an evil presence'.

There is a powerful illustration of this kind of experience in an unexpected place: Tim Smit's book about the restoration of the now famous gardens at Heligan in Cornwall. Tim Smit describes himself as a rationalist, but nevertheless tells the story of what happened when his colleague John Nelson was digging in an isolated area of the gardens known as the Tump. First of all John's dog started acting strangely. She raised her hackles and refused to go with him. Then John himself felt the hairs on the back of his neck stand up. He saw a huge, indefinable black shape apparently rise up out of the ground in front of him and then disappear among the trees. Pale and shaking, he reported what he had seen.

So, despite his rationalism, Tim Smit turned to the local vicar for help. When they came to the Tump, there on the ground, half hidden among the leaves, were bits of wood in the shape of a pentacle. It was evidently a site of satanic worship. Without knowing that or knowing why, both the dog and then John Nelson had sensed the evil in this place. The vicar prayed over the site in the name of Christ, and within only a few days people who didn't even know what had taken place – indeed, didn't know that anything had taken place – were reporting a lighter, happier atmosphere in the garden, the lifting of some kind of darkness.

Source: Adapted from David Hay, Exploring Inner Space (second edition, Mowbray, 1987), p 152; Tim Smit, The Lost Gardens of Heligan (Victor Gollancz, 1998), pp 210–215.

Bible references: Job 1:6–7; Matthew 4:1–11,24; 8:16,28–34; 9:32–33; 10:1,8; 12:22–29; 15:21–28; 17:14–18; Mark 1:23–27, 32–34,39; 3:11–15,22–27; 5:1–20; 6:7; 7:24–30; 9:17–27; 16:17; Luke 4:1–13,33–36,41; 8:26–39; 9:1; 10:17–20; 11:14–26; John 8:44; 12:31; Acts 5:16; 8:7; 16:18; 19:13–16; Ephesians 6:12; James 4:7; 1 Peter 5:8–9; Revelation 12:9–10.

103. HELL (Afterlife, Eternity, Heaven, Youth, Humour)

Miss Watson said to Huckleberry Finn, 'Why don't you try to behave?' Then she told me all about the bad place, and I said I wished I was there. She got mad then, but I didn't mean no harm. All I wanted was to go somewheres; all I wanted was a change, I warn't particular. She said it was wicked to say what I said; said she wouldn't say it for the whole world; *she* was going to live so as to go to the good place. Well, I couldn't see no advantage in going where she was going, so I made up my mind I wouldn't try for it. But I never said so, because it would only make trouble, and wouldn't do no good.

Now she had got a start, and she went on and told me all about the good place. She said all a body would have to do there was to go around all day long with a harp and sing for ever and ever. So I didn't think much of it. But I never said so.

Source: Mark Twain, The Adventures of Huckleberry Finn (Chatto and Windus, 1884), pp 4–5.

Bible references: Matthew 6:19–20; 16:27; 25:31–46; Luke 12:32–34; 2 Corinthians 5:10; Galatians 6:8–9; Philippians 3:20; Colossians 3:1–2; 2 Peter 1:10–11; 3:13–14; Revelation 5:8; 7; 14:2–3; 15:2–4; 19:1–9.

104. MISSING THE POINT (Belief, Dogs, Evidence, Faith, Miracles, Proof, Truth, Unbelief, Walking on water, Humour)

A man was out walking his dog one day, throwing sticks for it to fetch. When they came to a pond, the man threw the stick into the water. The dog ran over the surface of the water, picked up the stick, and brought it back. The man could hardly believe his eyes! So he threw the stick into the pond again, and again the dog walked over the water to bring it back.

The man looked round to find a witness, someone else to see this incredible thing, and he called over another man who was walking his dog by the pond. 'Watch this!' he said, and threw the stick into the pond. Once again the dog ran across the surface of the water, picked up the stick in its mouth, and brought it back. 'What do you think of that, then?' the owner said proudly. 'A shame, isn't it,' the other man replied. 'It looks like your dog can't swim.'

Source: Adapted from Gavin Reid, in The College of Preachers' Fellowship Paper 103, June 1997.

Bible references: Matthew 11:20–24; 13:13–15; Luke 16:27–31; John 10:24–26,31,38; 12:37–40; 14:10–11; 15:24; Acts 28:23–27; 2 Corinthians 4:3–4.

105. OPPOSITION (Church, Clergy, Curses, the Devil, Division, Evil, Intercession, Marriage, Media, Newspapers, Persecution, Prayer, Satanism, Spiritual warfare)

A twenty-nine-year-old woman who claims that she was involved in a satanic network for a number of years before becoming a Christian, describes how the satanists prayed and worked against the church.

> They had specific people that they were praying against; prominent Christians in the area and people who were opposing them. They placed curses on some, that they would fail, very disastrously, so that everything would be destroyed around them, and the obvious things about marriage, homes, jobs, plans, that if they were a real risk, something would happen to them. They particularly prayed that the marriages of church leaders would fail.
>
> Some group members were given the job of infiltrating local Christian churches. It was their task to try and identify any existing weaknesses and to work on those areas to try to destroy the church from within. They would slowly chip away, bringing dissent, or whatever, into the church, so that spiritually they were being broken down.
>
> They would work as a group. The people would go in and infiltrate the church and then report back, and the part of the group that was involved in that side would then start working on it.

This involved both ritual and prayer. Other methods employed were plaguing ministers with phone calls, spreading rumours about them, and writing letters attacking them in the local press.

Source: Adapted from Andrew Boyd, Blasphemous Rumours (Fount, 1991), pp 366–367.

Bible references: Matthew 5:11–12; 10:22; Mark 13:13; Luke 6:22–23; John 15:18–21; Ephesians 6:10–18; 1 Peter 5:8–9; 1 John 3:13.

106. POWER (Business, Cults, Happiness, Human nature, Life, Modern life, Morality, Pride, Selfishness, Success, Work)

Do you want to be successful? Robert Greene has written a self-help manual for those who want to be among life's winners – he's called it *The 48 Laws of Power*. The laws include the following:

- Never put too much trust in friends, learn how to use enemies.
- Conceal your intentions.
- Always say less than necessary.
- Court attention at all cost.
- Get others to do the work for you, but always take the credit.
- Avoid the unhappy and unlucky.
- Learn to keep people dependent on you.
- Crush your enemy totally.
- Do not commit to anyone.
- Play on people's need to believe to create a cult-like following.
- Discover each man's thumbscrew – everyone has a weakness.
- Be royal in your own fashion: act like a king to be treated like one.

And, in a fascinating piece of Scripture-twisting:

- Strike the shepherd and the sheep will scatter.

Greene adds: 'I hate to tell you, but the real fools are the ones who take the values of decency and morality too seriously. The need for power and control is the most elementary human need. There is something deep in the core of human beings – insecurity, vanity, the urge to dominate and survive – that will never change. Learn to get power and you will be a better, happier human being.'

Source: Adapted from The Daily Telegraph, 19 September 1998.

Bible references: Psalm 73; Zechariah 13:7; Matthew 11:25–26; 26:31; Mark 14:27; Luke 10:21; John 7:45–49; Romans 1:21–23; 1 Corinthians 1:25–31; 2:1–5; James 3:13–16.

107. PRAYER (Belief, Communism, Dictators, Disillusionment, Doubt, Evil, Faith, Hardship, Holocaust, Intercession, Jews, Judaism, Nazism, Science, Second World War, Secularism, Suffering, Unanswered prayer, Unbelief)

Rabbi Lionel Blue has written:

> Early on, I was acquainted with unemployment, the dole, cancer, Mosley and Hitler... I prayed for the speedy demise of the two last who were terrorising our little Jewish community. Their followers threw old people through windows and daubed insults on our houses. According to Grandma, if you prayed hard enough for something holy, it would happen. Well, it didn't! I saw their photos in a newspaper a few weeks later, flourishing like bay trees.
>
> As I had suspected since going to school, Grandma's medieval recipes didn't work for faith, only for food. So, holding the hand of my uncle, I marched with the Reds instead, because they were scientific and knew what the world was about.

Prayer didn't change anything in the material world around me. It was magic which didn't work, pre-scientific juju. This I still believe....

I am a post-Holocaust Jew, painfully aware of the wagonloads of human misery on their way to the camps and gas chambers. How many prayers must have been said or sobbed in them, which were never answered in any way that made sense to those who prayed them? A God who 'answers' the prayers of a neurotic like me, or the occasional sufferer at a shrine, but who didn't release those Jews from their misery is a God too frivolous and erratic to worship.

Source: Lionel Blue, My Affair with Christianity (Hodder and Stoughton, 1998).

Bible references: Malachi 2:17; 3:13–15; Luke 11:5–10; 18:1–8; 2 Peter 3:9.

108. SCIENCE (Astronomy, Belief, Christianity, Faith, Morality, Religion, Theology, Humour)

In a university common room, a professor of astronomy was having a go at the Christian faith. He said to a theology lecturer, 'Let's face it, basically all religions are the same, aren't they? I mean, what they all boil down to is the Golden Rule: treat other people as you'd like them to treat you.'

'I suppose that's one way of looking at it,' replied the theologian. 'Just as in astronomy it all boils down to one thing, really: "Twinkle, twinkle, little star".'

Source: Adapted from Calvin Miller, Spirit, Word and Story: A Philosophy of Marketplace Preaching (Baker Books, 1996), pp 165–166.

Bible references: Leviticus 19:18; Matthew 7:12; 22:39; Luke 6:31; Galatians 5:14; James 2:8.

109. SOCIETY (Belief, Communism, Faith, God, History, Modern life, Suffering, Unbelief)

In a lecture in 1983 the Russian writer Alexander Solzhenitsyn explained what he believed to be the root cause of Russia's troubles:

> More than half a century ago, while I was still a child, I recall hearing a number of old people offer the following explanation for the great disasters that had befallen Russia: 'Men have forgotten God. That's why all this has happened.' Since then I have spent well-nigh fifty years working on the history of our revolution; in the process I have read hundreds of books, collected hundreds of personal testimonies, and have already contributed eight volumes of my own toward the effort of clearing away the rubble left by that upheaval. But if I were asked today to formulate as concisely as possible the main cause of the ruinous revolution that swallowed up some sixty million of our people, I could not put it more accurately than to repeat: 'Men have forgotten God. That's why all this has happened.'

Source: Quoted in Haddon Robinson, ed., Biblical Sermons (Baker Book House, 1989), pp 247–248.

Bible references: Deuteronomy 4:5–9,23–24; 6:10–12; 8:10–20; 32:15–18; Judges 3:7; Psalms 9:17; 50:22–23; Isaiah 17:10–11; 51:12–13; 65:11–12; Jeremiah 2:31–32; 3:21; Hosea 13:6–9.

110. STANDARDS (Approval, Commitment, Discipleship, God, Judgement, Music, Popularity, Priorities, Self-esteem)

The story is told of a young pianist who was a musical prodigy. His talent was astonishing, and when news came that he was to visit London and play at the Royal Festival Hall the tickets sold out in no time. When the evening of the concert arrived the hall was packed. The audience was so expectant you could feel it in the air. And then the young man walked out on stage and sat at the piano. The atmosphere was electric, and the capacity crowd wasn't disappointed. The young man played brilliantly. From start to finish he played with such consummate skill and artistry that people were entranced. And as the last note of the last piece died away they rose to their feet as one and clapped until their hands were sore. The young man stood and bowed, and then made his way off the stage. The audience clapped still harder, and called out, 'Encore, encore.' In the wings the stage manager looked at the pianist. 'Aren't you going back on?' he asked. 'Listen to them calling for you.' 'No,' said the young man, 'I don't think I played at my best tonight.' 'Oh come, come,' said the stage manager, 'That's not what the audience thinks. Look, they're all on their feet applauding.' 'No they're not,' argued the pianist. 'They are,' replied the stage manager, 'Just look at them!' So the young man pointed to a box high up beside the stage. 'Look there,' he said. 'That man's not clapping.' And sure enough, in the midst of all the cheering, clapping figures on their feet, there was one elderly man still sitting in his seat.

'He's probably deaf!' retorted the stage manager. 'Or unmusical. Or even dead! Surely you're not going to refuse to go back on just because one old man won't stand up?' 'You don't understand,' replied the pianist. 'That's my piano teacher. He knows I didn't play my best tonight.'

Source: Adapted from Steve Chalke, International Congress of Preachers 1997.

Bible references: John 5:41–44; 7:18; 8:49–50; 12:43; Galatians 1:10; 1 Thessalonians 2:4–6; Hebrews 12:1.

THE BIBLE

111. ADAM (Books, Creation, History, Innocence, Nakedness, Navel, Science, Sects, Theology, Humour)

The English Civil War, a time of political and religious upheaval, saw the emergence of a whole range of weird and wonderful religious sects. One group was known as the Adamites because they apparently believed themselves to have regained the state of innocence from before the fall. As a result they worshipped – like Adam and Eve before the fall – in a state of utter nakedness!

One question which probably didn't bother the Adamites, but which did trouble the minds of some serious-minded scholars, arose from Adam's unique position of having not had a mother. In 1857 Philip Gosse, a distinguished naturalist, wrote a book called *Omphalos: An Attempt to Untie the Geological Knot. Omphalos* is Greek for a navel, and Gosse's question was this: since Adam had not been born, did he have a navel? Anatomically, he obviously didn't need one, but Gosse decided that theological considerations were more important: since God created Adam in every respect like his descendants, he would indeed have had one!

Source: Adapted from Christopher Hibbert, Cavaliers and Roundheads (HarperCollins, 1993), p 26; R.J. Berry, God and Evolution (Hodder and Stoughton, 1988), p 104.

Bible references: Genesis 2:7,25.

112. AMAZING DISCOVERIES (Armageddon, Conspiracy theories, Dead Sea Scrolls, End Times, False prophets, Gullibility, Media, Millennium, Newspapers, Prophecy, Revelation, Tabloids, Vatican, Virgin birth, Humour)

The Vatican has been suppressing the explosive revelations contained in the Dead Sea Scrolls. At least, that's what the American tabloid newspaper the *Sun* claimed in its edition of 11 June 1996. In a world exclusive, the *Sun* revealed that secret files in the Vatican contained what it called in its banner headline the 'Lost Prophecies of the Dead Sea Scrolls'. These included the following predictions:

- in the year 1998 Jesus would be reborn to a virgin in Idaho;
- in 1999 scientists would succeed in eliminating all known diseases through a new wonder drug made from olive stones;
- in 2000 a great storm lasting 100 days would unleash a second world-wide flood, killing millions.

According to the newspaper, church officials had kept these scrolls hidden because they 'deemed these prophecies too controversial for the masses'. In a follow-up story on 24 September 1996, the paper quoted a so-called 'biblical expert' named Dotson Meade, supposedly from London, who said:

> The Dead Sea Scrolls spell out a frightening Armageddon and the enlightenment that comes after it. One [date] clearly points to 2000 and even shows the specific day as August 13. Another date specifies July 7, 2077... Many of us believe following Christ's battle with and victory over Satan in 2000 we will enjoy the spiritual Heaven-on-Earth promised us. But in 2077 the inhabitants of earth will leave this planet and migrate to others.

So now you know....

Source: Adapted from Biblical Archaeology Review, September–October 1996; January–February 1997.

Bible references: Revelation 19:11–21; 21.

113 BOOKS (Culture, Literature, Modern life, Secularism)

The Folio Society offered its fifty thousand members a list of fifty books and asked them to say which had exercised the most significant influence on their lives. When the votes were counted, pride of place went to J.R.R. Tolkien's fantasy *The Lord of the Rings*, which was judged the most influential book. The Bible came in at number thirty-five, sandwiched betwen *Don Quixote* and Flaubert's novel of provincial adultery, *Madame Bovary*. Writing in the Bible Society's magazine, *TransMission*, Dan Beeby commented, 'Ironically, rejected by many as legend and myth, the Bible lost out to fable, fantasy and fiction. From being the Book of books around which Europe was fashioned, it now ranks below *The Wind in the Willows* and *Cold Comfort Farm*.'

Source: Adapted from TransMission, Spring 1998.

Bible references: Jeremiah 8:9; Amos 8:11–12; Matthew 22:29; Mark 12:24; John 5:39; Romans 15:4; 2 Timothy 3:15–17; Hebrews 4:12.

114. COMMANDMENTS (Amazing discoveries, Gullibility, Media, Newspapers, Prayer, Sickness, Tabloids, Women, Humour)

On 9 April 1996, the American tabloid newspaper the *Sun* reported that 'the discovery of a second sensational set of Ten Commandments has stunned theologians and historians around the world'. The new set is said to have been found, alongside a set of the original ten, on a mountain in Saudi Arabia. Closer inspection reveals that the new commandments don't quite come up to the moral and ethical standard of the ten with which we are more familiar. For example, number 11 states, 'Thou shalt discover everlasting life in the herbs that grow'; number 15 says, 'Thou shalt honour women, for in the eyes of the Lord they are blessed', and number 16 declares, 'Thou shalt use the power of prayer to heal thyself of all sickness.' On the positive side, at least they sound easier to keep!

Source: Adapted from Biblical Archaeology Review, January–February 1997.

Bible references: Exodus 20:1–17; Deuteronomy 5:6–21; Mark 10:19; Luke 18:20.

115. JESUS (Belief, Christ, Families, Forgiveness, Healing, Judaism, Kingdom of God, Law, New Testament, Poverty, Prophecy, Rabbis, Sabbath, Sin, Temple, Wealth)

When Christians read the New Testament we try to understand why many Jews rejected Jesus as the

Messiah. Rabbi Dan Cohn-Sherbok, who is Professor of Judaism at the University of Wales in Lampeter, has written about why practising Jews still reject Jesus as their Saviour today. And he shows that things haven't changed much in two thousand years. He gives six principal reasons.

First, he says, and most important, for the Jewish community it is clear that Jesus didn't fulfil the expectations of the Messiah which are recorded in the Old Testament, in postbiblical literature, and in the teaching of the rabbis. He didn't restore the kingdom of David, he didn't gather in the scattered people of Israel, he didn't restore all the laws of the Torah, nor did he rebuild the temple and renew the whole of creation.

Second, the claim that Jesus enjoyed a special relationship with God (he quotes Matthew 11:27 and John 14:6–7) runs counter to the Jewish conviction that everyone is equal before God.

The third objection relates to Jesus' attitude towards sin and sinners. The Old Testament prophets used to take Israel to task for rejecting God's law; they didn't offer people forgiveness. So Jesus put himself above the prophets in claiming to have the power to forgive what only God could forgive. No wonder the people around Jesus were shocked when he said, 'Your sins are forgiven' (eg Matthew 9:5–6, Luke 7:48–49). This was usurping God's prerogative, and it was unprecedented.

Another problem is Jesus' attitude to poverty, which he seems to say is a good thing (eg Matthew 19:21, Luke 6:20). In Jewish eyes, poverty is an evil, and wealth is a blessing.

A fifth aspect of Jesus' teaching with which Jews are unhappy is his demand that his followers should be willing to break all family ties (Cohn-Sherbok cites Luke 14:33, Matthew 12:48–50 and 23:9). In Judaism, where the family is so important, to break it up is seen as a travesty of the created order.

Finally, Jesus' teaching is rejected by Jews because his interpretation of Jewish law runs counter to rabbinic tradition. The example that Rabbi Cohn-Sherbok gives is his healing on the Sabbath. Several times Jesus cured people on the Sabbath who were not dangerously ill, which violates the rabbinic precept that the Sabbath law can only be broken for the saving and preserving of life (he quotes Matthew 12:9–14; Luke 13:10–16; 14:3–6).

So the rabbi sees Jesus in much the same way as his contemporaries did, 'as one preacher among many, a false Messiah who had failed to fulfil the scriptural predictions of redemption and deliverance.' Little has changed in two millennia.

Source: Adapted from The Church of England Newspaper, 12 December 1997.

Bible references: Matthew 9:5–6; 10:37; 11:27; 12:1–14,47–50; 19:21–24; 23:9,23–24; 26:63–66; Mark 2:9–11,23–28; 3:1–6,32–34; 10:21–25; 14:61–64; Luke 5:23–24; 6:1–11,20,24; 7:48–49; 8:19–21; 11:42; 12:33–34; 13:10–16; 14:1–6,26,33; 18:22–25; John 5:1–18; 7:22–24; 8:54–59; 9:13–16; 10:14–15,30–33; 14:1–7,10–11; 16:15,19–31; 17:20–23.

116. NUMBERS (Church Fathers, Interpretation, Learning, New Testament, Scholarship, Humour)

Many people know about the huge range of opinions that have been put forward over the ages about the significance of the number of the beast in Revelation – 666 – but it may come as a surprise to discover how much scholarly ink has been spilt about the number of fish caught by the disciples in John 21:11, namely 153.

Jerome was one of the first to offer an explanation.

He said that ancient writers had believed that there were 153 different species of fish in the world, and so the number represented all the nations of the world. Augustine had a different theory. He noted that 153 was a 'triangular' number, that is, the sum of the numbers from 17 downwards. Ten was the number of the commandments, Revelation refers to the sevenfold Spirit of God, and 10 + 7 = 17. One modern scholar has gone down a similar line, pointing out that when 5,000 were fed in John 6, five loaves of bread were taken and twelve baskets left over, and 5 + 12 = 17.

Other academics prefer the approach which is so beloved of the interpreters of 666, giving numerical values to each letter: the numbers chosen vary according to the interpreter. On this basis scholars have come up with phrases such as 'the church of love' (even though this is a phrase not found in the writings of John!), 'the children of God', or even 'Cana G' – short, of course, for Cana in Galilee, the site of the first miracle recorded by John. An even more involved interpretation is one which involves reversing the usual numerical order, so that, in English, Z would equal 1, and so forth. On this reading, 153 would be made up by IXΘ, an abbreviation of *Ichthus*, which was an early Christian code for Jesus Christ, Son of God, Saviour. Evidently this scholar believed that John would have enjoyed cryptic crossword puzzles!

Among many others, too many to mention, we might also take note of the suggestion put forward by the medieval scholar Rupert of Deutz. He suggested that the number represents the fullness of the church: 100 represents the married, 50 the widows, and 3 the virgins. None of these interpreters gives serious consideration to another possibility, that is, that there were actually 153 fish in the net!

Source: Adapted from G.R. Beasley-Murray, John (Word, 1987), pp 102–103; D.A. Carson, The Gospel According to John (IVP, 1991), pp 672–673.

Bible references: John 21:11; Revelation 13:11–18.

117. RELIABILITY (Ancient history, Archaeology, Interpretation, Old Testament, Translation, Weights and measures)

The Hebrew text of 1 Samuel 13:21 included a word which puzzled translators for a long time. The word is *pim*. The King James Version translated it as 'file' (for sharpening), but that was pure guesswork: nobody really knew what a *pim* was. But during the twentieth century achaeologists excavating sites such as Timnah, Ashdod and Ekron discovered some small dome-shaped weights inscribed with the Hebrew word *pim*. So now we know what a *pim* was: about a quarter of an ounce of silver, or two-thirds of a shekel. This was what the Philistines charged the Israelites to sharpen their ploughshares or mattocks.

What is so significant about this particular discovery is that these weights are found only in strata from the ninth to seventh centuries BC, after which the *pim* apparently disappeared. That makes it highly likely that 1 Samuel – or at least a version of it – was written during that period, rather than in the second century BC, as some critics have suggested, five hundred years after the weight had vanished from circulation.

Source: Adapted from Biblical Archaeology Review, September–October 1996; Neal Bierling, Giving Goliath his Due (Baker Book House, 1992), pp 142–143.

Bible references: 1 Samuel 13:21.

118. REMEMBERING (First World War, History, Old Testament, Philistines, War)

In its account of Israel's battles against the Philistines, 1 Samuel 14 describes an incident at Michmash, a strategically important site which guards the entrance to the Israelite highlands. A Philistine detachment was occupying a hilltop site of about half an acre, protected from Saul's army by cliffs which they evidently believed to be too steep to climb. Guided by God, Jonathan and his armour-bearer climbed the rock-face, attacked the Philistine outpost, and killed about twenty men. This threw the rest of the Philistine forces into panic and confusion, so that they were easily routed by the main body of the Israelite army.

During the First World War the Turkish army was occupying the area around Michmash, and British forces were ordered to move forward and capture it. It is said that a staff officer dimly remembered the Bible story. He looked it up, and went to his commanding officer, General Allenby, to read him the account. Scouts were sent to find the trail that Jonathan might have used, one leading up to a half-acre plot on high ground. They found a pass between two cliffs, one facing towards Michmash and the other towards Geba, just as the Bible described. A detachment of troops was sent up the trail under cover of darkness, surprised the Turkish troops at the top, and as a result the Turkish army, a short distance away, was routed, just as the Philistines had been so many centuries earlier.

Source: Adapted from Neal Bierling, Giving Goliath his Due (Baker Book House, 1992), pp 146–147.

Bible references: 1 Samuel 14:1–23.

119. REVELATION (666, Antichrist, Computers, End times, History, Interpretation, Millennium, New Testament, Numbers, Politics, Pope, Reformation, Humour)

Every generation has read the book of Revelation in the light of its own times, and interpreted – or perhaps we should say misinterpreted – it accordingly. For instance, if you were a sixteenth-century Protestant, you were told that the Pope was the antichrist; if you were a Catholic, you were shown how the name Martin Luther made 666. In the seventeenth century, many English people still thought that the papacy was the antichrist, but the Puritans claimed that it was the Church of England hierarchy, and the extreme radicals thought that it was Oliver Cromwell himself. At the end of the eighteenth century, some Englishmen thought Napoleon was the antichrist, while in the Americas others thought King George III fitted the bill.

During the twentieth century speculation ran riot. In the 1920s some saw Mussolini as the obvious candidate to be the antichrist, others said it was the League of Nations, and then Hitler became the favourite (especially when it was discovered that his name could be made to equal 666 by taking A = 101, B = 102, etc.). After the war some saw the United Nations as the beast, others thought it was NATO, but in the 1970s Hal Lindsey popularised the idea that it was the European Community. This was made more problematic when the Community grew to include fifteen members by the 1990s, but mere details have never discouraged millennarian speculation. As for the antichrist, several American presidents have been suggested (from John F. Kennedy at one end of the political spectrum to Ronald Reagan at the other), various popes (from Pius XII to John Paul II), bogeymen like Mikhail Gorbachev and

Saddam Hussein, and a range of other figures as diverse as Henry Kissinger, Sun Myung Moon, the Spanish king Juan Carlos, or even Bill Gates of the Microsoft corporation (if A = 6, B = 12, etc., Computer = 666!).

Source: Simon Coupland.

Bible references: Revelation 13:11–18.

120. SABBATH (Interpretation, Jesus, Judaism, Law, Mishnah, New Testament, Pharisees)

The Mishnah identified thirty-nine different kinds of work which were prohibited on the Sabbath (7.2). As a result, when Jesus' disciples plucked grain and ate it on the Sabbath, they were breaking the Law in a whole host of ways. From a Pharisaic perspective, they had reaped (plucked the grain), winnowed (rubbed it between their hands), threshed (separated the chaff), and prepared a meal (eaten the grain).

The penalties for Sabbath-breaking could be strict. The book of Jubilees specified the death penalty for anyone who went on a journey, farmed, rode a beast, lit a fire, travelled by ship, killed a beast or caught a fish on the Sabbath (50.12).

Centuries of debate had worked out how to apply the Law to a whole variety of everyday situations. Thus *Shabbath* 3–6 in the Mishnah lays down that on the Sabbath:

- a new lamp can be moved from one place to another, but not an old one;
- hot food may be kept warm by covering it with clothes, feathers, or dried flax, but not with damp herbs or straw (because they might engender heat, which would constitute work);

- an ass may go out wearing its saddle cloth, but only if it has been put on before the Sabbath;
- it may not wear a bell, even one that has been muffled, because that would count as work;
- goats may go out with a protective cloth over their udders as long as it is only to keep them dry, and not to collect the milk.

And to show how carefully the scribes had thought of every eventuality, *Shabbath* 10.3 specified that a man could not carry a burden 'in his right hand or in his left hand, in his bosom or on his shoulder'. But he was permitted to carry something 'on the back of his hand, with his foot or his mouth or his elbow, or in his ear or his hair, or in his wallet, carried mouth downwards, or between his wallet and his shirt, or in the hem of his shirt, or in his shoe or sandal'.

Source: Adapted from Robert Mounce, Matthew (Hendrickson, 1991), pp 111–112; Michael Green, Matthew for Today (Hodder and Stoughton, 1988), p 74; Leon Morris, Luke (IVP, 1988), p 225.

Bible references: Exodus 20:8–11; 23:12; 31:12–17; 34:21; Deuteronomy 5:12–15; Nehemiah 13:15–22; Jeremiah 17:19–22; Matthew 12:1–14; 23:23–24; Mark 2:23–28; 3:1–6; Luke 6:1–11; 11:42; 13:10–16; 14:1–6; John 5:1–18; 7:22–24; 9:13–16.

121. SABBATH (Dead Sea Scrolls, Essenes, Interpretation, Jesus, Judaism, Law, New Testament, Qumran)

We know that the Pharisees were strict regarding Sabbath observance, but the Dead Sea Scrolls reveal that their sect (probably but not certainly the Essenes) were even more scrupulous. Here are some of the Sabbath prohibitions in the so-called Damascus Document (4Q266–272):

- if you have made a loan, you cannot ask for repayment on the Sabbath;
- not only may you not do any work or any form of business, you cannot even discuss what you intend to do the next day;
- nor can you cheat by getting a Gentile to do your business for you;
- you may not carry anything, either outdoors or indoors, because that counts as work, even if it is someone else's baby or your own medicine;
- you are only allowed to eat what has previously been prepared.

The same document also contains various provisions laying down what is permitted and what is not in certain specific circumstances:

- if you are on a journey and go down to the river to wash, you are allowed to drink the water, but not to scoop it up with a bottle or a flask;
- you can take your animal up to 2,000 cubits outside the town to graze, but you may not use force. If it doesn't want to go, it has to be left at home.

And some of the rules provide an obvious contrast to the teaching of Jesus:

- if an animal gives birth on the Sabbath, nobody is allowed to help it; if it falls into a well or a pit, nobody can lift it out;
- if a person falls into a well or into water, nobody is allowed to use a ladder or a rope to help them get out.

Source: Adapted from Michael Wise, Martin Abegg, Jr., and Edward Cook, trans., The Dead Sea Scrolls: A New Translation (HarperCollins, 1996), pp 68–69.

Bible references: Exodus 20:8–11; 23:12; 31:12–17; 34:21; Deuteronomy 5:12–15; Nehemiah 13:15–22; Jeremiah 17:19–22; Matthew 12:1–14; 23:23–24; Mark 2:23–28; 3:1–6; Luke 6:1–11; 11:42; 13:10–16; 14:1–6; John 5:1–18; 7:22–24; 9:13–16.

122. TEMPLE (Herod, Jesus, Judaism, New Testament)

When Jesus' disciples exclaimed, 'Look, Teacher! What massive stones! What magnificent buildings!' it is easy for us to underestimate just how massive and how impressive the Temple complex was.

The platform on which the Temple stood was enormous: the largest of its kind in the ancient world. The southern wall, the shortest, was 930 feet long, the western wall, the longest, 1,620 feet long. The Temple Mount thus enclosed an area the size of some thirteen football pitches, two and a half times as long as St Peter's Basilica in Rome, and nearly four times as wide. By way of comparison, it was five times the area of the Acropolis in Athens.

The smallest of the stones used to build the massive walls weighed between two and five tons, and many weighed ten tons or more. The majority were 3–4 feet high, and between 4 and 10 feet long, though some stones were much, much larger. Those which are still in place on the south-west corner are about 40 feet long, 3 feet high, and 8 feet thick, and weigh about 50 tons each. A number of massive stones in the western wall are unequalled in size anywhere in the ancient world. The largest is almost 40 feet long, 10 feet high, and 13 feet thick, and must weigh around 400 tons.

Two thousand years later, these walls are still as solid and sturdy as if they had just been built. At the joins where the blocks meet, we can see that they have not moved at all in that time, not even a millimetre. Sometimes it is only the dressing around the edge of the stones that shows where one block ends and the next begins.

Source: Adapted from Meir Ben-Dov in Hershel Shanks and Dan P. Cole, eds, Archaeology in the World of Herod, Jesus and Paul (Biblical Archaeology Society, 1990), pp 21–30; Alan Millard, Discoveries from the Time of Jesus (Lion, 1990), pp 88–90.

Bible references: Matthew 24:1–2; Mark 13:1–2; Luke 21:5–6.

123. TRANSLATION (Art, History, Interpretation, Misinterpretation, Mistakes, Misunderstanding, Old Testament)

Visitors who make the pilgrimage to San Pietro in Vincoli church in Rome to see Michelangelo's magnificent statue of Moses are frequently puzzled by the two horns on the prophet's head. Was the sculptor trying to suggest there was something demonic about Moses? The answer is that Michelangelo was working from the Catholic Church's authorised Latin translation of the Bible, the Vulgate, in which Exodus 34:29 was mistakenly translated, 'Moses did not know that his face was horned' (Latin: *cornuta*). The King James Version, by contrast, correctly translated: 'that the skin of his face shone'.

A similar kind of mistake can be found in the ninth-century Stuttgart Psalter, which in the illustration accompanying Psalm 78 shows little dogs climbing up the corn and eating the ears. This is because the text mistakenly describes one of the plagues of Egypt as 'caniculae' – little dogs – and the artist wanted to be faithful to Scripture, odd though it must have appeared to him.

Source: Simon Coupland.

Bible references: Exodus 34:29; Psalm 78:46.

124. WORD OF KNOWLEDGE (Gifts of the Spirit, Guidance, Poetry, Humour)

The American preacher James Ryle often has words from God. He tells how a friend of his was once approached by a man asking him for a word from the Lord. His friend gave the man a Bible and said, 'Here is a whole book of words from the Lord. Read it!'

In a similar but slightly different vein, it is said that a Christian once went up to the poet Sir John Betjeman and gave him a piece of paper with a poem written on it. 'The Lord gave me this poem,' he said. Betjeman read the poem, then tore up the paper and threw it away with the comment, 'The Lord has given and the Lord has taken away. Blessed be the name of the Lord.'

Source: Adapted from James Ryle, Hippo in the Garden (Highland, 1992), p 67; Hilary Brand in Renewal, July 1998.

Bible references: Job 1:21; Matthew 15:6; Mark 7:13; John 10:35; 1 Corinthians 12:8; 13:2; 14:6, 26–32; Ephesians 6:17; 2 Timothy 3:15–17; Hebrews 4:12.

THE CHURCH

125. BODY OF CHRIST (Churchgoing, Commitment, Criticism, Service, Humour)

A clergyman who was preaching on the body of Christ drew attention to a few parts of the body which St Paul hadn't mentioned. Some of the congregation were like the tonsils, he said, because, 'We're no worse off when you're gone.' Others were like the appendix: 'We didn't notice you were there until you started grumbling.' And others were like a set of false teeth, 'Sometimes in and sometimes out.'

Source: Adapted from W.E. Sangster, The Craft of Sermon Construction (Marshall Pickering, 1989), p 98.

Bible references: Romans 12:4–5; 1 Corinthians 12:12,14–27; Ephesians 4:11–12,15–16; Colossians 2:19.

126. CHURCH AND STATE (Deception, God, Militarism, Nazism, Patriotism, Propaganda, War)

The belt buckles of the German soldiers who fought in the Second World War read 'Gott mit uns': God with us. They made the claim that God was on the German side. What was worse, as we can see with the benefit of hindsight, was that the church establishment supported them in this belief. For example, four days after Hitler's armies invaded Russia in June 1941, the Roman Catholic bishops in Germany issued a pastoral letter to be read out by the clergy in every church across the nation. It said this:

> In this grave hour for the Fatherland, which is having to wage a war of unparalleled extent on broad fronts, we admonish you to do your duty loyally, to endure bravely, to be ready for sacrifice, and to fight in the service of our people. We send a greeting of grateful love and deep blessing....
>
> As you fulfil the onerous duty of this time, in the harsh tribulations which will come upon you as a result of the war, may you be strengthened by the comforting certainty that you are doing God's holy will.

Source: Quoted in Günther Weber, I Believe, I Doubt (SCM, 1998), p 195.

Bible references: Jeremiah 5:31; 6:14; 8:11; 14:14–16; 23:33–38; 29:8–9; Lamentations 2:14; Ezekiel 13:1–16; 22:28; Micah 3:11; Zechariah 10:2; Matthew 7:15–20.

127. CRITICISM (Discernment, Discipline, Hospitality, Listening, Monks, Will of God, Humour)

According to an old story, there's a monastery in Italy with the following sign in it:

> First, if a stranger comes to this monastery, you will share with him what you have.
> Second, if he criticises, listen. He may be sent by the Lord.

Third, if he becomes obstreperous, he shall be cast out.
Fourth, if he refuses to go, four strong monks shall explain to him the will of God.

Source: Quoted in Calvin Miller, The Empowered Leader (Broadman and Holman, 1995), pp 38–39.

Bible references: Romans 12:13; 1 Timothy 6:18; Hebrews 13:2,16; 1 Peter 4:9.

128. FASTING (Abstinence, Alcohol, Brothers, Families, Lent, Pubs, Humour)

A barmaid was bemused by the fact that every Wednesday a man came into the pub, ordered three pints, then went to a table by himself where he sat and drank them one after the other. Eventually she couldn't contain her curiosity any longer and asked him why he did it. He explained to her that he used to go out for a drink every Wednesday with his two brothers, but now they'd gone overseas, and so they'd all agreed that wherever they were, they would go out for a drink on a Wednesday and buy three pints, one for each of them, and drink each other's health.

The barmaid thought this was rather touching, and so she was a bit worried when a few months later, just before Easter, the man ordered just two pints. When he did it again the following week, she plucked up courage and said to him, 'I hope you don't mind me asking, but I do hope nothing's happened to one of your brothers.' 'Oh, no,' he said, 'It's not that. No, you see, I've given up alcohol for Lent.'

Source: Adapted from Christopher Hamel Cooke, A Time To Laugh (Arthur James, 1993), pp 31–32.

Bible references: Matthew 6:16–17; 9:14–15; Mark 2:18–20; Luke 5:33–35; Acts 13:2–3.

129. GRACE (Christianity, Guilt, Intolerance, Jesus, Love, Prejudice, Respectability, Sin)

A Christian in Chicago who worked with street people was approached by a prostitute who was in a desperate situation. She didn't know he was a Christian, she just knew him as someone who might be able to help. She described the mess she was in: she was sick, she was a drug addict, she was homeless, and she had a two-year-old daughter that she couldn't even afford to buy food for. And with tears running down her face she admitted that in her desperation she had even gone so far as to sell her little girl for sex to pay for drugs. The man was horrified, but he tried not to let it show. He asked her if she had ever thought of going to a church for help. She looked at him in complete amazement. 'Church!' she said, 'Why would I ever go there? They'd just make me feel even worse than I already do!'

How far we have come from the teacher who was criticised as a friend of outcasts and sinners.

Source: Adapted from Philip Yancey, The Jesus I Never Knew (Zondervan, 1995), pp 147–148.

Bible references: Matthew 9:10–13; 11:19; 21:28–32; Mark 2:15–17; Luke 5:29–31; 7:34,36–50; 15:2; 18:9–14; 19:7,10.

130. HOLY COMMUNION (Bible, Faith, Prayer, Reflection, Silence, Space flight, Unity)

In July 1969 Neil Armstrong and Buzz Aldrin stepped into the history books when they became the first people ever to set foot on the moon. That part of the story is well known. Less well known is what Buzz Aldrin did to mark the momentous achievement of landing safely on the moon.

> Our powered descent was right on schedule. With only seconds of fuel left, we touched down at 3.30pm. Now was the time for communion.
>
> I unstowed the elements in their flight packets. I put them and the Scripture reading on the little table in front of the abort guidance-system computer. Then I called Houston. 'Houston, this is Eagle. This is LM Pilot speaking. I would like to request a few moments' silence. I would like to invite each person listening in, wherever and whoever he may be, to contemplate for a few moments the events of the past few hours, and to give thanks in his own individual way.'
>
> For me, this meant taking communion. In the blackout I opened the little plastic packages which contained bread and wine. I poured wine into the chalice my parish had given me. In the one-sixth gravity of the moon, the wine curled slowly and gracefully up the cup. It was interesting to think that the very first liquid ever poured on the moon, and the first food eaten there, were consecrated elements.
>
> Just before I partook the elements, I read the words which I had chosen to indicate our trust that as a man probes into space, we are in fact acting in Christ. I sensed especially strongly my unity with our church back home, and with the church everywhere.
>
> I read, 'I am the vine; you are the branches. Whoever remains in me, and I in him, will bear much fruit; for you can do nothing without me.'

Source: Quoted in SALT magazine for All-Age Worship (Scripture Union), April–June 1997. Copyright © Buzz Aldrin, Scripture Union 1997. Reproduced by kind permission of Scripture Union.

Bible references: Matthew 26:17–30; Mark 14:12–26; Luke 22:7–20; John 15:1–5; 1 Corinthians 11:23–25.

131. HOW OTHERS SEE US (Advertising, Boredom, Communication, God, Modern life, Morality, Relevance, Theology, Youth)

Comedian Jo Brand wrote in the *Independent*:

> There's been some controversy about a new batch of posters attempting to attract younger people into the church. The posters have used language which, it was felt, would appeal more to young people. But apparently the more traditional Christians have not been pleased by phrases like 'bad hair day' – not to mention what they consider to be a rather flippant summing-up of the Nativity story.
>
> This is the problem with the church. For want of a better phrase, it is so holier-than-thou. I've always thought God probably doesn't give a toss about the sort of language you use, providing you don't go round torturing animals or battering your neighbours. The main obstacle for young people in the church is not the initial advertising dilemma, but surely the point at which they actually arrive at church to discover the services are dull, interminable and of very little relevance to contemporary life.

Source: Quoted in The Chichester Magazine, December 1996. Reproduced by kind permission of Jo Brand.

132. HOW OTHERS SEE US (Churchgoing, Communication, Evangelism, Gospel, Hypocrisy, Modern life, Relevance, Witness, the World)

What do people outside the church think of it? The well-known publicist Max Clifford is pretty blunt. 'My view of the church is buildings and small attendances, and when I read and hear from church people, the general thought that goes through my mind is that they are out of touch. I'm totally unaware of what the church has been doing to change its image, to reinvent itself. It might just be that I've missed it. But from the general perspective, my friends and the people I'm involved with come from wide circles, and the word "church" never seems to figure anywhere these days.'

He believes that the church consists mostly of elderly people who look smart and act 'holier than thou'. 'I'm not a cynic,' he says, 'but the kind of people I know that go to church wouldn't do anything for anybody. They are only interested in themselves and once they are out of that building, they can be the most ruthless, dictatorial and corrupt people.'

And his solution to the church's image problem? To find new ways of communicating and living out the gospel. 'I believe that people gain from hearing good news, they feel better about themselves, life and the community. The church has got to show that it is alive, effective and caring going into the next century, not just among the people who go to church.'

Source: Adapted from The Church of England Newspaper, 6 March 1998.

133. MUSIC (Change, Choirs, Criticism, Disagreement, Division, Intolerance, Organ music, Prejudice, Quarrels)

Church music has always been changing, and has always been a bone of contention. For instance, a contemporary of Johann Sebastian Bach wrote in 1732, three years after Bach had written his St Matthew Passion:

> When in a large town his Passion music was performed for the first time, with twelve violins, many oboes, bassoons and other instruments, many people were astonished and did not know what to make of it. In the pew of a noble family in church, many ministers and noble ladies were present, who sang the first Passion chorale out of their books with great devotion. But when this theatrical music began, all these people were thrown into the greatest bewilderment, looked at each other and said, 'What will become of this?' An old widow of nobility said, 'God save us, my children! It's just as if one were at an opera comedy!' But everyone was genuinely displeased by it and voiced just complaints against it. There are, it is true, some people who take pleasure in such idle things.

The move to introduce the organ into churches in New England in the late eighteenth century provoked equally bitter opposition. A church in Boston was first offered an organ by the treasurer of Harvard University in 1713, but turned it down on the grounds that 'if organs were permitted, other instruments would soon follow, and then there would come dancing'! Eventually the church ordered an organ from England at the end of the century, but even as the instrument was being shipped across the Atlantic, the congregation was still bitterly divided. One wealthy member offered to reimburse the entire cost of the organ if only the thing were thrown to the bottom of Boston harbour, sparing the house of God from desecration.

Source: Adapted from Ministry, September 1996.

134. PREDESTINATION (Afterlife, Damnation, Election, Exclusiveness, Heaven, Hell, Intolerance, Judgement, Prejudice, Salvation)

An old Particular Baptist hymn supposedly goes like this:

> We are the Lord's elected few,
> Let all the rest be damned;
> There's room enough in hell for you,
> We won't have heaven crammed.

Source: Spring Harvest notes 1995, p 86.

Bible references: Matthew 7:13–14,21–23; Luke 13:24–25; 15:25–30; 18:9–14.

135. THE WAY WE WERE (Bishops, Christianity, Church of England, History, Nostalgia, Secularism)

We all too often assume that in the eighteenth and nineteenth centuries the church was flourishing, confident and influential. In fact this was far from the case, as the following quotations show.

- In 1709 Dean Jonathan Swift wrote, 'Hardly one in a hundred among our people of quality or gentry appears to act by any principle of religion; great numbers of them do entirely discard it, and are ready to own their disbelief of all revelation in ordinary discourse. Nor is the case much better among the vulgar.'

- At about the same time the Bishop of St Asaph, William Beveridge, remarked, 'Doctrine and precepts are so generally slighted and neglected... So little of Christianity is now to be found among Christians themselves: to our shame be it spoken.'
- In 1722 Daniel Defoe commented, 'No age, since the founding and forming of the Christian church in the world, was ever like (in open avowed atheism, blasphemies and heresies), to the age we now live in.'
- In 1747 Bishop Butler refused the Archbishopric of Canterbury, saying, 'It is too late to try to save a failing church.'
- In the following century, Thomas Arnold wrote in 1832, 'The church as it now stands no human power can save.'
- And in 1880 Bishop Ryle observed, 'The Church of England today is in a more critical and perilous position than at any period in the last two centuries. We are in rough waters, and whether or not we will weather the storm remains to be seen.'

Source: Quoted in A. Skevington Wood, The Burning Heart (Paternoster, 1967), p 12, and in Nigel McCulloch, Barriers to Belief: Steps to a Stronger Faith (Darton, Longman and Todd 1994), pp 42–43.

Bible references: Ecclesiastes 7:10.

136. WITNESS (Christianity, Evangelism, Faith, Gospel, Hypocrisy, Intolerance, Joy, Lifestyle, Searching, Unbelief)

Bertrand Russell was well known for his lack of Christian faith. His daughter later wrote:

> I would have liked to convince my father that I had found what he had been looking for, the ineffable something he had longed for all his life. I would have liked to persuade him that the search for God does not have to be in vain. But it was hopeless. He had known too many blind Christians, bleak moralists who sucked the joy from life and persecuted their opponents; he would never have been able to see the truth they were hiding.

Source: Quoted in Dancing in the Dark? (Lynx, 1994), p 58.

Bible references: Matthew 6:22–23; 7:3–5; 9:12–13; Luke 5:31–32; 6:41–42; 11:34–36; 15:25–30; 18:9–14.

137. WORSHIP (Copyright, Music, Songs, Humour)

At a church where they use an overhead projector they put up the words of a new song. They went like this:

Jesus, Jesus, Jesus
Jesus, Jesus, Jesus
Jesus, Jesus, Jesus.
Repeat twice.

And underneath it said: Words copyright.

Source: Michael Perham, Bath 1995.

BISHOPS AND CLERGY

138. ACCOUNTABILITY (Adultery, Affairs, Alcohol, Church, Clergy, Denominations, Drugs, Leadership, Magic mushrooms, Management, Ministry, Reports, Supervision, Humour)

When Eugene Peterson became pastor of a new church, he had to send monthly reports on his work to a denominational committee in New York. The first part was statistical: how many people attended worship, how many visits he had made, what shape the finances were in, and so on. The second part was a theological reflection on his ministry. After a few months he began to get the impression that nobody was reading this, so he decided to check it out.

The next month he filled in all the statistics, but then described how he was suffering from depression. He couldn't sleep, he said, and couldn't pray. He was seriously questioning whether he should be a pastor at all. Did the committee have any suggestions? In fact, none of this was true. He'd made it all up to see if it would provoke a response, but he heard absolutely nothing.

So the next month he raised the stakes. He admitted that he'd got a drinking problem, which had got so bad that one Sunday he hadn't been able to finish the sermon. He felt he needed treatment – could the committee help? Once again there was no reply. So the next month he confessed that he'd been having an affair. It had all started innocently enough, he said, when he'd been counselling a woman in a difficult marriage, but suddenly things had got out of hand and he'd ended up making love to her on one of the pews. What was worse, at that moment one of the flower arrangers had walked in! He wrote that he'd been afraid that his ministry was ruined, but that to his surprise the congregation had actually doubled the following Sunday, as news had got round.

Still there was no response whatsoever, so the next month he described how he had put magic mushrooms in the communion wine. This was the 1960s, when somebody had suggested that the Jesus movement was really a mushroom cult, so Peterson said that he'd tried the theory out on his congregation. It had been a fantastic experience, he said, and incredible worship, but he wasn't sure whether there were any denominational rules about it. Could they please advise him?

After three years, the supervision ended, and he was invited to New York to discuss how he'd got on. He said that he was rather disappointed that they had never read his reports. 'Oh but we did!' the committee answered. 'We read those reports carefully; we take them very seriously.' So Eugene Peterson asked them why they hadn't helped him with his depression, or his drink problem, why they hadn't taken any action over his affair or his use of magic mushrooms. When they looked at him completely blankly, he knew – and they knew – that he had them over a barrel.

Source: Adapted from Eugene Peterson, Under the Unpredictable Plant (Eerdmans, 1992), pp 77–79.

Bible references: 1 Corinthians 4:2; 2 Timothy 2:15; Hebrews 13:17; James 3:1.

139. ADULTERY (Affairs, Blackmail, Clergy, Counselling, Discernment, Ministry, Sin, Temptation)

A pastor in California was counselling a woman who was suffering from depression. The sessions seemed to go well: she was obviously benefiting from their time together, and he was encouraged. Then one day she phoned up and said that she couldn't come to their appointment, she was too down, but could he come round to her house and see her? Against his better judgement, he went. As soon as he got through the door, she fell into his arms in floods of tears, and naturally he put his arms around her to comfort her. She responded, and soon she started cuddling him and caressing him. One thing led to another, and before long they ended up in bed together. At that moment the cupboard door opened, a man stepped out and took a picture.

The minister realised he was going to be blackmailed. To his credit, he went straight to the police, and the couple were arrested. But his ministry in that place was over, and he knew it.

Source: Adapted from Calvin Miller, Disarming the Darkness (Zondervan, 1998), p 123.

Bible references: Exodus 20:14; Deuteronomy 5:18; Proverbs 2:12–19; 6:23–33; 7:7–27; Romans 2:22; 13:13; 1 Corinthians 5:9–13; 6:18–20; 10:8; Ephesians 5:3; Colossians 3:5–8; 1 Thessalonians 4:1–8; 5:22; 1 Timothy 3:1–13; 4:12; Titus 1:6–9; 2:6–7.

140. BISHOPS (Clerical dress, Forgetfulness, Old age, Pride, Humour)

A bishop was making a pastoral visit to an old people's home in his diocese, as usual wearing his purple cassock and a big cross around his neck. He went up to one elderly lady, sitting in her chair, and asked her how long she'd been living there. 'Why do you want to know?' she snapped.

He carried on regardless, 'Do you have your own room?'

'Go away and leave me alone!' she said.

The bishop wasn't used to this kind of response. 'Do you know who I am?' he asked.

'No, I don't,' she said, 'But I'm sure if you ask the matron, she can tell you.'

Source: Simon Coupland.

141. BISHOPS (Accidents, Air travel, Confidence, Faith, Flying, Humour)

Norman Vincent Peale was once flying on an aeroplane when the Captain's voice came over the loudspeaker: 'We need to inform you that one of our engines has shut down, but the other three will enable us to complete our journey.' Then he added, 'To reassure any of you who might be worried, let me tell you that we have four Methodist bishops on board today.' A woman sitting beside Peale called a stewardess over and said, 'With the greatest respect, could you please tell the Captain that I'd be far happier if there were three bishops and four engines.'

Source: Quoted in David Wilkinson and Rob Frost, Thinking Clearly About God and Science (Monarch, 1996), pp 48–49.

142. CHURCH (Afterlife, Belief, Bishops, Christ, Church of England, Clergy, Heresy, History, Myth, Nostalgia, Reputation, Resurrection, Unbelief)

There is nothing new under the sun, including criticism of the standard of the clergy, as these quotations show.

- In the sixteenth century John Calvin said that many of the bishops of his day declared that 'there is no God... that everything written and taught about Christ is incorrect and misleading... that the doctrines of a life to come and of a final resurrection are mere myths'.
- In the seventeenth century Lucius Cary, the Member of Parliament for Newport, said, 'They who hated bishops hated them worse than the devil, and they who loved them did not love them so well as their dinner.'
- In the eighteenth century, the great open-air preacher George Whitefield was becoming so popular that some of King George II's courtiers are said to have suggested to the king that something should be done to restrain him. The king reportedly joked, 'I believe the best way will be to make a bishop of him!'
- In the nineteenth century, Edward King, the newly appointed Bishop of Lincoln, was told that the clergy of his diocese 'could be divided into three categories: those who had gone out of their minds, those who were about to go out of their minds, and those who had no minds to go out of.'

Source: Adapted from Alister McGrath, Roots that Refresh (Hodder and Stoughton, 1992), p 94; Christopher Hibbert, Cavaliers and Roundheads (HarperCollins, 1993), p 29; John Pollock, George Whitefield and the

Great Awakening (Lion, 1986), p 231; A.N. Wilson, ed., The Faber Book of Church and Clergy (Faber and Faber, 1992), pp 241–242.

Bible references: Ecclesiastes 7:10; Ezekiel 34:1–6; 2 Timothy 4:3–4.

143. CONFIRMATION (Bishops, Churchgoing, History, Nostalgia, the Way we were)

In the nineteenth century, when so many more people were confirmed, on at least one occasion the Bishop of Norwich confirmed a thousand children in a single service. The churchwardens carried a long plank covered with purple cloth to the bishop. The bishop stood up, placed both hands on the plank, and then the three of them slowly walked down each aisle. As the plank passed over them, the children bowed their heads and were deemed to be duly confirmed, even if the bishop's hand never did actually touch their heads!

Source: Adapted from a review of Ronald Blythe, Word from Wormingfold: A Parish Year, in The Daily Telegraph, 5 April 1997.

144. FOOT IN MOUTH (Baths, Bishops, Class, Cleanliness, Hygiene, Misunderstanding, Humour)

Arthur Winnington Ingram, who was Bishop of London at the beginning of the twentieth century, was obsessive about cleanliness, and often took two or three baths a day. When he was visiting the East End of London he tried to convince the working classes that it was good for them to wash frequently, and at one point he made the mistake of saying, 'Why, after a bath I feel rosy all over!' Some cockney wag at the back shouted, 'An' 'oo's Rosie, then?'

Source: Canon Alan Wilkinson in Canterbury Tales (Channel Four, 1996).

145. HOLY WATER (Accidents, Animals, Clergy, Death, Healing, Miracles, Raising the dead, Humour)

A Catholic priest was driving a devout but simple member of his congregation along a country road in Ireland one day when he accidentally ran over a hare. He stopped the car, and the two men got out and walked over to where the animal was lying. It wasn't moving, and looked to be dead. But then the priest went back to the car and fetched a bottle from a bag he had in the boot. He opened the bottle and sprinkled a few drops of liquid on the hare. It immediately twitched and started coming round. He then sprinkled a few more drops on it and it sat up, looked around, and then lolloped away.

His passenger was amazed. 'My goodness, Father,' he said, 'That must be powerful holy water you've got with you!'

'Not at all,' replied the priest. 'It's common or garden hare restorer.'

Source: Adapted from Sir Gawain Bell, in Pass the Port (Christian Brann, 1976), p 28.

Bible references: 1 Kings 17:17–24; 2 Kings 4:18–37; Matthew 9:18–25; Mark 5:22–43; Luke 7:11–15; 8:41–56; John 11:1–44; Acts 9:36–41; 20:9–12.

146. HUMILITY (Bishops, Clergy, Death, Discipleship, Goodness, Grace, Mercy, Ministry, Modesty, Pride, Sin)

When Cardinal Basil Hume, the leader of the Roman Catholic Church in England, was told that he had terminal cancer, his first thought was, 'If only I could start all over again, I would be a much better monk, a much better abbot, a much better bishop.' But then he reflected, and he said, 'Then I thought, how much better if I can come before God when I die, not to say, "Thank you that I was such a good monk, good abbot, good bishop," but rather, "God be merciful to me a sinner". For if I come empty-handed, then I will be ready to receive God's gift. God be merciful to me a sinner.'

Source: From the funeral address by the Right Reverend John Crowley, Bishop of Middlesbrough, quoted in The Daily Telegraph, 26 June 1999.

Bible references: Proverbs 16:18–19; 25:27; 26:12; Micah 6:8; Matthew 18:1–4; Luke 5:8; 18:9–14; Romans 12:3; 1 Corinthians 4:6–8; 13:1–3; Galatians 6:3–5; Philippians 2:3–8; James 4:6; 1 Peter 5:5–6.

147. THE MEDIA (Bishops, Church, Materialism, Misquotation, Money, Newspapers, Preaching)

A bishop was preaching on the evils of materialism. 'You must never think you are in this world solely for the purpose of making money,' he thundered. This was good newsworthy stuff, and the sermon was reported by the press. Unfortunately someone added a full stop in a critical place, so that the bishop was reported to have said: 'You must never think. You are in this world solely for the purpose of making money.'

Source: Adapted from John G. Murray, A Gentleman Publisher's Commonplace Book (John Murray, 1996), p 57.

Bible references: Matthew 6:24; 19:23–24; Mark 10:25; Luke 6:24; 16:13; 18:24–25; 1 Timothy 6:9–10,17.

148. MOVING ON (Choir, Church, Churchwardens, Committees, Day off, Deacons, Elders, Leadership, Ministry, Missionaries, PCC, Preaching, Humour)

All clergy have their ups and downs. Sometimes, however, things get so bad that it's probably time to think about moving on. I've written this from an Anglican perspective, but if you are – or have – a pastor rather than a vicar, simply adjust 'wardens' to 'elders' or 'deacons', and 'PCC' to eldership, committee, or whatever.

It's time to think about moving on when:

- You wake up from a dream in which you're preaching a terrible sermon – and find that you are.
- You're the only one to turn up to a bring-and-share supper.
- The missionary committee gives you plane tickets to visit all the church's missionaries, staying a month with each.
- The churchwardens ask you to change your day off – to a Sunday.
- You're asked to go on the crèche rota – and the children are out during the whole service.
- The fabric committee agree to create more car parking space – by tarmacking over your front lawn.
- The choir get up to sing the next hymn just as you get up to preach.
- The PCC send you a get well card – by a one vote majority.

Source: Adapted from Edward K. Rowell and Bonne L. Steffen, Humor [sic] for Preaching and Teaching (Baker Books, 1996), pp 194–196, 210–211.

149. THE GOOD OLD DAYS (Baptisms, Church, Clergy, Funerals, History, Laziness, Ministry, Nostalgia, Pastoral care, Visiting, Weddings, Work)

'Of course you only work one day a week' is the kind of comment guaranteed to annoy the clergy. But in the eighteenth century it really could be a cushy job, to judge by the meticulously kept diaries of the Revd James Woodforde, Vicar of Weston Longueville in Norfolk. In the year 1791 he took just one service each Sunday, as well as an extra service on Good Friday. In addition, he officiated at fourteen christenings, six churchings (for the purification of women after childbirth), two weddings and eleven funerals. There were, after all, only 360 souls in the parish. Even so, in the course of the year just one sick visit doesn't seem many. He didn't take any services for clergy in neighbouring parishes, although he did attend the bishop's and archdeacon's visitations. Michael Hinton adds, 'A clergyman has, of course, duties other than public ones, notably those of private devotion, study and sermon preparation. So far as the evidence Woodforde provides allows us to judge, he did not spend great tracts of time on any of the three.'

Source: Adapted from Michael Hinton, The Anglican Parochial Clergy, a Celebration (SCM, 1994), p 313.

Bible references: Ecclesiastes 7:10; Ezekiel 34:1–6; 1 Timothy 4:13–15; 2 Timothy 2:15.

150. THEOLOGY (Academics, Doubt, Faith, Learning, Light, Scepticism, Scholarship, Humour)

The eighteenth-century atheist French philosopher Denis Diderot wrote: 'Wandering in a vast forest at night, I have only a faint light to guide me. A stranger appears and says to me, "My friend, you should blow out your candle in order to find your way more clearly." This stranger is a theologian.'

Source: Diderot, Additions aux Pensées philosophiques (c.1762), quoted in John Gross, The Oxford Book of Aphorisms (Oxford University Press, 1983), p 15.

Bible references: Proverbs 26:12; Ecclesiastes 12:12; Matthew 15:14; Luke 6:39; Romans 16:17–18; 1 Corinthians 8:1–2; Galatians 1:6–9; 1 Timothy 1:3–7; 6:3–5; 2 Timothy 4:3–4.

151. VISITING (Clergy, Dogs, Embarrassment, Ministry, Politeness, Humour)

A new vicar was still settling into his parish, and he decided that a good way to get to know his congregation was to visit them all in their homes. One afternoon he was making his rounds, but as he approached the next house on his list his heart sank. There, sitting on the front doorstep, was a Rottweiler. He summoned up all his courage, sidled past the dog, and rang the bell. The dog didn't make a move, and when the lady of the house opened the door and invited the vicar in, the dog got up and followed.

The visit went well, the vicar drank his tea and enjoyed getting to know the family, but he was a little shocked when the dog stood beside the sofa, cocked its leg, and did its business. But since the family said nothing, he thought he'd better not either, and the conversation carried on.

A little while later the vicar got up to leave, and said his goodbyes. But just as he was going out of the door, the lady called after him, 'Aren't you going to take your dog with you?'

Source: Adapted from The Church of England Newspaper, 20 December 1996.

PREACHERS AND THEIR SERMONS

152. BOREDOM (Banns, Misunderstanding, Weddings, Humour)

In order to get married by banns in an Anglican church, at least one of the couple has to be resident in the parish where the service is to take place. So at the turn of the century one young man was asked by the vicar, 'Do you sleep in the parish?' The answer wasn't quite what he'd expected. 'Yes, sir,' the young man replied, 'I've slept through several of your sermons.'

Source: Adapted from P.H. Ditchfield, The Old-time Parson, quoted in A.N. Wilson, ed., The Faber Book of Church and Clergy (Faber and Faber, 1992), p 157.

Bible references: Acts 20:9–12.

153. BOREDOM (Bequests, Church, Dogs, Wills, Humour)

John Rudge, who lived at Trysull in Staffordshire in the eighteenth century, evidently sat through more than his fair share of dull sermons. In his will of 17 April 1725 he wrote: 'I do also bequeath the sum of twenty shillings a year, payable at five shillings a quarter, to a poor man to go about the parish church of Trysull, during sermon, to keep people awake, and to keep dogs out of the church.'

Source: Quoted in Tombstone Humour (Chancellor Press, 1993), p 146.

Bible references: Acts 20:9–12.

154. DISCOURAGEMENT (Boredom, Clergy, Frustration, Humility, Listening, Ministry, Priorities, Visiting speaker, Humour)

Preaching can be a discouraging business.

Stuart Briscoe once preached at a series of meetings in South Carolina over the course of a week. At the end of the week there was a question and answer session in which people had the chance to ask about anything that he'd said. There was only one question. It came from an elderly lady who had sat in the front row every night. She wanted to know: 'Is them your own teeth?'

Or again, Haddon Robinson recalls an occasion when he spoke as a visiting preacher and felt that the sermon had really gone down well. After the service he was standing at the back of church waiting for the pastor when he noticed a pew card that someone had written on. It said, 'I wonder how long this guy's going to preach. There's going to be a long line at the cafeteria.'

Source: Adapted from Stuart Briscoe, in Mastering Contemporary Preaching (Multnomah Press, 1989), p 170; Haddon Robinson, in A Voice in the Wilderness (Multnomah Press, 1993), p 27.

Bible references: Proverbs 4:20–22; Ezekiel 33:31; 2 Timothy 4:2; James 1:22–24.

155. EVANGELISM (Culture, Discouragement, Encouragement, Gospel, Gullibility, Mission, Missionaries, Politeness, Witness, Humour)

In the 1950s, an American evangelist working in Japan called Glenn Wagner managed to get permission to show a gospel film to the police cadets in the city of Nagoya. The plan was that first he would show the film, which was called *God's Creation*, then he or someone else would preach, a Japanese Christian would give his testimony, then Wagner would invite the cadets to give their lives to Christ. There were 500 cadets, but the cinema where the film would be shown could only seat 250, so the cadets were split into two batches.

At the first showing the cadets listened politely enough, but when it came to Wagner's evangelistic appeal, nobody responded. Not a single one of the cadets put his hand up to show that he wanted to come to Christ. Wagner was really discouraged.

Just before the second meeting, the Japanese Christian who was going to give his testimony happened to be in the projection room sorting out the film when the cadets came in. As the American hadn't yet arrived, the chief of police gave them a talking-to. 'Yesterday,' he said, 'When the missionary asked for a show of hands, nobody responded. We need to make this man happy because we want a good relationship with the United States.'

When the end of the meeting came, and the evangelist asked if anyone wanted to give their life to Christ, every hand in the room went up. He could hardly believe it. He went away and wrote an enthusiastic report about how revival was breaking out in Japan. If only he knew!

Source: Adapted from G.W. Prange, D.M. Goldstein and K.V. Dillon, God's Samurai (Brassey's [US], Inc., 1990), pp 230–231.

Bible references: Isaiah 29:13; Matthew 13:24–30,36–43; 15:8; Mark 7:6; John 2:23–24; 6:14,26–27,64.

156. FUNERALS (Accidents, Commitment, Death, Decisions, Evangelism, Insensitivity, Judgement, Life, Manipulation, Truth)

Will Willimon tells of the time when he was a young minister in rural Georgia, and a member of his congregation asked him to go to a relative's funeral. He says:

> I had never seen a funeral like that! They had the body out there in the church, the casket was open, the preacher started preaching and he preached and he preached, and the gist of his sermon was something like, 'It's too late for Joe. He's dead! You can look at him: he's dead! But it is not too late for you.' Then the preacher told us about various disasters he'd read about recently. There was a funeral procession in another state and this bus ran through the funeral procession and killed a bunch of people: 'That could happen to you this afternoon! Joe might have wanted to give his life to God, he might have wanted to change his life, he might have wanted to do something: he can't, he's dead now.'
>
> I sat there thinking, 'I know this is a comfort to this family.' I had never seen anything like this. I couldn't believe it. 'Now is the day for decision,' he said. 'Now! You could die tonight, in bed. Don't forget the bus coming through the funeral procession. Now is the time to give your life to God. One day it will be too late for you: you'll be like Joe.'
>
> On the way home, I said to my wife, 'That was the most insensitive, manipulative, tacky thing I have ever seen in my life. Could you believe that guy?' She agreed it was insensitive, it was manipulative, it was tacky, and she said, 'You know, the worst part about it is, it was true. It really was too late for him. And it's not too late for us.'

Source: Will Willimon, International Congress of Preachers, London 1997.

Bible references: Matthew 7:21–23; 25:1–13; Luke 13:24–30; Acts 2:37–40; 2 Timothy 4:2; Hebrews 4:1–2,11; 12:25; Jude 22–23.

157. GUIDANCE (Calling, Discernment, Interpretation, Ministry, Visions, Vocation, Will of God, Humour)

R.T. Kendall, the minister of Westminster Chapel, tells of one of his friends who was out ploughing corn in the fields one day when he saw the clouds in the sky above him form the letters 'PC'. He immediately realised that the Lord was telling him to 'Preach Christ'. So in obedience to the message, he gave up ploughing corn and started preaching Christ. R.T. adds that some of his congregation later suggested that perhaps what the Lord was really saying was, 'Plough corn'!

Source: Adapted from R.T. Kendall, Ready for God? (Scripture Union, 1995), p 117.

Bible references: Genesis 15:1; 46:2; 1 Kings 19:19–21; Jeremiah 1:4–14; Daniel 2:19–23; Amos 7:1–9,15; 8:1–2; Matthew 4:18–19; 9:9; Mark 1:16–18; Luke 9:62; Acts 9:10–16; 10:9–17; 16:9–10; 18:9–10; 1 Corinthians 9:16–17.

158. HONESTY (Brothers, Building programmes, Character, Church, Clergy, Compromise, Death, Funerals, Hypocrisy, Judgement, Lifestyle, Lying, Money, Morality, Respectability, Saints, Sin, Truth, Humour)

There were once two brothers who made lots of money from their shady dealing. They were corrupt, they were immoral, but they were clever, too, so they managed not to get caught. And they set great store by their apparent respectability.

One of the many people whom they didn't succeed in fooling was the local clergyman. He knew exactly what was going on and what kind of people they were, even if he didn't make a point of saying so publicly.

All of a sudden one of the brothers died. And the clergyman was naturally asked to take the funeral. During the funeral visit, the surviving brother took out his chequebook and said, 'Now, vicar, I know the church is always short of money, and I know how much you need to replace your roof. Here's a cheque for twice that amount, on one condition. At my brother's funeral I want you to say that he was a saint.'

The minister promised that he would do so, and banked the cheque.

On the day of the funeral, to everyone's surprise, he really let rip. 'You all know what this man was like,' he said. 'He was a liar, a cheat and a crook, and he never did an honest deal in his life. Mind you,' he went on, 'compared to his brother, he was a saint!'

Source: Adapted from Anna Marano and Steve Wallace, Worthing 1998.

159. RELEVANCE (Application, Bible, Clergy, Life, Old Testament, Priorities, Work, Humour)

Spurgeon once said of a type of preacher, 'He is great upon the ten toes of the beast, the four faces of the cherubim, the mystical meaning of badgers' skins, and the typical bearings of the staves of the ark, and the windows of Solomon's temple; but the sins of the businessman, the temptations of the times, and the needs of the age, he scarcely ever touches upon.'

Source: Quoted in Calvin Miller, Spirit, Word and Story: A Philosophy of Marketplace Preaching (Baker Books, 1996), p 71.

Bible references: Exodus 25:5,13–15,27–28; 26:14; 27:6–7; 30:4–5; 34:34; 35:7,12–16,23; 36:19; 37:4–5,14–15,27–28; 38:5–7; Numbers 4:6–14,25; 1 Kings 6:4; Ezekiel 1:6,10,15; 10:14,21; Daniel 2:41–42.

160. REPETITION (Bible, Clergy, Harvest, Ministry, New minister, Humour)

The new vicar had just arrived and people were looking forward to hearing him preach his first sermon. He got up in the pulpit and said, 'I'd like to speak to you today about one of my favourite passages in the Scriptures, the episode in the garden of Gethsemane where Peter cuts off the ear of the high priest's servant.' And he went on to preach what they all agreed afterwards was a jolly good sermon.

The following week they looked up expectantly as he climbed into the pulpit, so they were a bit taken aback when he began with precisely the same introduction: 'I'd like to speak to you today about one of my favourite passages in the Scriptures, the episode in the garden of Gethsemane where Peter cuts off the ear of the high priest's servant.' And he went on to preach exactly the same sermon as the week before, word for word. After the service there was a bit of muttering, but people agreed that he'd only just moved in, and he must have been busy unpacking and sorting himself out, so they could understand that perhaps he hadn't had time to write a fresh sermon. They'd see what happened the following Sunday.

The next week exactly the same thing happened. The same introduction, the same sermon. But by now people were beginning to feel that something ought to be said, especially as the following week was harvest festival. So one of the churchwardens agreed to have a word with the vicar. 'We do appreciate your sermons, vicar,' he said, diplomatically, 'but we were wondering, as next Sunday is harvest festival, whether you could preach on something topical, something on the harvest theme.' 'Of course,' replied the vicar, 'Just leave it to me.'

So the following Sunday there was particular expectancy as the vicar stood in the pulpit and opened the Bible. 'My text for today,' he began, 'comes from the fourth chapter of St Mark's Gospel, and the twenty-eighth verse. "The earth produces of itself, first the blade, then the ear." And that reminds me of one of my favourite passages in the Scriptures.... '

Source: Adapted from Peter Sertin, Paris 1981.

Bible references: Matthew 26:51–52; Mark 4:28; 14:47; Luke 22:49–51; John 18:10.

161. SECRETS (Clergy, Criticism, Eggs, Husbands, Marriages, Wives, Humour)

There was once a clergyman who fell in love with a girl, and asked her to marry him. She agreed, on two conditions. The first was that he should never ask how much she spent at the hairdresser's, the second that he should never look inside the box which she would keep under the bed. He readily agreed to the two conditions, and not long afterwards they got married.

They lived together very happily for over twenty years. Many a time the husband noticed the wooden box peeping out from under their bed, but true to his word, he never opened it and never tried to peek inside it. He never even picked it up and rattled it.

But then one day, the wife had gone out to the hairdresser's when the clergyman had to pop upstairs to fetch a dog collar. Imagine his surprise when he walked into the bedroom and saw the box lying open on the bed. His wife must have forgotten to put it back when she went out. Naturally, he couldn't help seeing what was inside it. There were two things. The first was an egg box, an ordinary cardboard egg box, with four eggs in it. The second was a roll of banknotes: at a rough guess he reckoned there must have been about £2,000. He left everything just as it was and went back downstairs.

When his wife came in, she immediately ran upstairs to the bedroom, then walked slowly back down again. 'Have you been upstairs?' she asked.

'I have.'

'Into our bedroom?'

'Yes.'

'Did you see what's in the box?' she asked.

'I did.'

'And you'd never looked before?'

'No,' he answered, quite truthfully.

'Oh well,' she said, 'after all these years I don't suppose it matters.'

But now her husband couldn't contain his curiosity. 'Tell me,' he said, 'why on earth do you keep a box of eggs under our bed?'

'I may as well tell you,' she said. 'It's like this. Every time you preach a bad sermon I put an egg in the box.'

The clergyman thought to himself, 'That's amazing. We've been married for over twenty years, and in all that time she thinks I've only preached four bad sermons! What a wonderful wife I've got.'

Then she carried on, 'And every time the egg box is full, I sell the eggs and put the money I get in the box.'

Source: Unknown.

162. SERMONS (Clergy, Criticism, Humour)

The curate asked the vicar what he thought of his sermons.

The vicar thought for a moment and said, 'They're like diamonds.'

'Really?' said the curate, who was delighted, 'Like diamonds?'

'Yes,' the vicar answered, 'If you want to make them sparkle, first you've got to cut them and then you've got to polish them.'

Source: Simon Coupland.

163. THE TONGUE (Application, Bible, Church, Discipleship, Lifestyle, Humour)

A preacher got up to preach one Sunday, and he had a big sack in his hand. (This is a true story!) He told the congregation, 'I have in this bag the most dangerous thing in the world.' He put his hand into the bag and pulled out a knife. Not just a little kitchen knife but a great big machete. He swung it round his head, chopped the air with it, and talked about the terrible things that people had done with knives and swords. Then he said, 'But the most dangerous thing in the world is not a knife.' And he put the knife down.

He reached into the bag again and pulled out a pistol. He pointed it at the ceiling and fired. Five hundred Baptists rose into the air as one, and sat back down again. The preacher talked about the awful things that had been done with guns, the wars, the crimes, the murders, but then he said, 'Guns are not the most dangerous thing in the world,' and put the gun down.

Then he reached into the bag again and pulled out a cow's tongue. He'd got it from a butcher's shop. It was disgusting, repulsive, hideous. He walked down to the people in the pews and held it out to show them. People were feeling nauseous. But then the preacher, whose name was Jim Burns, said, 'This, my brothers and sisters, is the most dangerous thing in the world. Can a fountain send forth bitter water and sweet?' And so he began a sermon on the book of James, about the power of the tongue.

Source: Adapted from Calvin Miller, International Congress of Preachers, London 1997, and his book, The Empowered Communicator (Broadman and Holman, 1994), pp 122–123.

Bible references: James 3:3–12.

164. WAR (Church, Church and state, Clergy, History, Military service, Patriotism, Politics)

Peter Muhlenberg's congregation never forgot his final sermon. Muhlenberg was an Anglican minister in Virginia in the 1770s, the time when the American colonies were debating whether to throw off British rule. Muhlenberg himself was an outspoken advocate for the rights of the colonies, saying that he would never confuse 'invoking a divine blessing on the king with wearing a parliamentary yoke'.

He was in St John's Church in Richmond in 1775 when Patrick Henry urged the Virginia militia to take up arms, ending his speech with the immortal cry, 'Give me liberty or give me death!' Muhlenberg was so moved that he immediately enlisted under George Washington, and returned to his own church to preach his farewell sermon.

He announced as his text Ecclesiastes 3:1, and declared, 'There is a time to preach and a time to pray, but there is also a time to fight, and that time has now come!' With that, he threw off his robes to reveal the uniform of a colonel in the militia underneath. He then recruited the men of his congregation to join him in the revolutionary army. Together they formed the German Regiment, which Muhlenberg commanded throughout the War of Independence, ending up as a major general. And his congregation never forgot that final sermon.

Source: Adapted from Christian History, issue 50.

Bible references: Ecclesiastes 3:1–8.

165. WITNESS (Boldness, Challenge, Conversion, Evangelism, Gospel)

Tony Campolo was once at a prayer breakfast where he was sitting next to the state governor. During the course of the conversation it became clear that the governor was very sympathetic to Christianity but had never actually made a Christian commitment. 'Why not?' Tony Campolo asked him.

'No one ever asked me,' said the governor.

'Well, I'm asking you,' said Campolo.

And to his surprise and delight, the governor replied, 'OK, I will.' And there and then he gave his life to Christ. Sometimes we just need to speak up.

Source: Adapted from Leighton Ford, in Changing Lives Through Preaching and Worship (Moorings, 1995), p 73.

Bible references: Acts 24:24–25; 26:28–29; Colossians 4:3–6; 2 Timothy 4:2; 1 Peter 3:15.

MODERN LIFE

166. COMMUNICATION (Grace, Jargon, Language, Preaching, Witness, the World)

This is a true story. Two people were talking across the aisle in a bus one day. One of them, a young woman, was reading M. Scott Peck's best-selling book about the meaning of life, *The Road Less Travelled*.

'What are you reading?' the man opposite her asked.

'A book a friend gave me,' the woman answered. 'She said it changed her life.'

'Oh yeah?' said the man, 'What's it about?'

'I'm not sure yet,' she said. 'Some sort of guide to life. I haven't got very far yet.' She flipped through the book. 'Here are the chapter titles: Discipline, Love, Grace... '

The man interrupted her, 'What's grace?' he asked.

'I don't know,' the woman answered. 'I haven't got to Grace yet.'

When we in the church talk about grace, we shouldn't assume that anyone else outside has a clue what we're on about.

Source: Adapted from Philip Yancey, What's So Amazing about Grace? (Zondervan, 1997), p 29.

Bible references: John 1:14–17; Romans 1:7; 1 Corinthians 1:3–4; 2 Corinthians 1:2; 8:9; 12:9; 13:14; Galatians 1:3; Ephesians 1:2;

2:4–8; Philippians 1:2; Colossians 1:2; 1 Thessalonians 1:1; 2 Thessalonians 1:2; 1 Timothy 1:2; 2 Timothy 1:2; Titus 1:4; Philemon 3; Hebrews 4:16; 13:25; 1 Peter 1:2; 2 Peter 1:2; 2 John 3; Revelation 1:4.

167. COMPUTERS (Communication, Forgiveness, Gender, Grudges, Human nature, Husbands, Marriage, Men, Sex, Technology, Wives, Women, Humour)

A committee was formed to decide whether computers should be thought of as male or female. The outcome was that the committee was split right down the middle, with the men arguing one way and the women the opposite. These were the reasons they put forward:

The men claimed that it was obvious that computers are female…

1. Because their internal workings are incomprehensible to everybody except their creator.
2. Because they communicate with each other in a language that no one else can understand.
3. Because as soon as you acquire a particular model you discover it needs all sorts of additional accessories.
4. Because their error messages don't help to solve the problem, whether it's 'Invalid command – please try again', or 'If you can't see why I'm angry I'm certainly not going to tell you!'
5. Because even when you delete a particular file you find that a backup copy has been stored away for later retrieval.

On the other hand, the women argued that computers are clearly male…

1. Because they contain a large amount of data but are still essentially clueless.
2. Because they are supposed to help solve problems but half the time are the problem themselves.
3. Because as soon as you acquire a particular model you discover that if you had waited you could have got a better one.
4. Because to get their attention you need to turn them on.
5. Because big power surges knock them out for the rest of the night.

Source: Adapted from John Hughes, New Wine 1998.

168. COMPUTERS (Abraham, Bible, Faith, Old Testament, Technology, Humour)

Abraham wants to upgrade his PC to Windows 98, and Isaac can't believe it. 'You've got to be crazy, Dad,' he says. 'You can't run Windows 98 on your old 386 model, everyone knows you need at least a fast 486 with a minimum of 16 megabytes of memory.' But Abraham, the man of faith, gazes calmly at his son and says, 'Don't worry, my son. God will provide the RAM.'

Source: Kevin Gibbs, Stanford in the Vale.

Bible references: Genesis 22:1–14; Hebrews 11:17–19; James 2:21.

169. DRIVING (Cars, Clergy, Highway Code, Hymns, Insurance, Music, Road safety, Humour)

Clergymen should definitely avoid making jokes about women drivers. Insurance company statistics show that ministers of religion have the highest record of insurance claims, an honour they share (for some unknown reason) with fishermen.

Perhaps that's why the Christian Road Safety Association commissioned some new hymns about road safety. One of the hymns includes the following lines:

> Whatever else we do each day,
> We strive to keep ahead.
> We try to turn the other cheek;
> Stop when the light is red.
> Obey the Hghway Code.

Honestly!

Source: Quoted in Tear Times, Spring 1997.

Bible references: Matthew 5:39; Luke 6:29.

170. HOW OTHERS SEE US (Church, Evangelism, Home groups, Neighbours, Reputation, Witness, the World, Humour)

In 1997 someone wrote to *The Sunday Times* problem page with the following dilemma:

> We recently moved house and want to be friendly with our neighbours. They seem nice and have invited us to a party. However, I have discovered that it is actually a meeting of their Christian fel-

lowship group. We ought to go to encourage good relations, but don't really want to mix with such people. What should we do?

NS, Godalming

What kind of reputation have we Christians acquired to drive people to write letters like that? Thankfully, the paper's agony aunt (or uncle) told 'NS' not to worry, adding, 'Committed Christians may be tiresome[!], but as far as I know they are not yet a dangerous cult bent on brainwashing new recruits.' Well, that's a relief.

Source: Adapted from The Sunday Times, 26 January 1997.

Bible references: 2 Corinthians 8:21; Colossians 4:5–6; 1 Thessalonians 4:12; 1 Timothy 3:7; Titus 2:7–8; 1 Peter 2:12,15; 3:13–16; 4:14–16.

171. INSTRUCTIONS (Consumers, Gullibility, Human nature, Stupidity, Humour)

Manufacturers evidently believe that it is impossible to overestimate the stupidity of the ordinary consumer. For instance, on the side of a packet of Sainsbury's peanuts it says: 'Contains nuts'. An American airline went still further. On the sachet of peanuts that passengers were given was written the message: 'Instructions: Open packet, eat contents.'

These aren't exceptional cases, to judge by an international list drawn up by *New Scientist* with the help of users of the Internet. For instance, a bottle of flavoured milk warns the buyer: 'After opening, keep upright.' A Swedish chainsaw manufacturer gives the advice: 'Do not try to stop chain with hands.' On one of their puddings, Marks and Spencer state, fairly enough: 'Product will be hot after heating.' Rowenta, who make irons, feel the need to tell the people who buy their products: 'Do not iron clothes on body.' And a camera on sale in Europe says: 'This camera only works when there is a film inside.' The journalist who reported the story, John Hoyland, commented: 'Either companies think we are really stupid – or people really are stupid.'

Source: Adapted from The Daily Telegraph, 27 December 1997.

172. THE INTERNET (Absolution, Church, Clergy, Computers, Forgiveness, God, Idols, Knowledge, New Religious Movements, Ordination, Saints, Science, Sin, Technology, Worship)

A canon of Bradford Cathedral, Geoff Smith, is one of the growing number of people across the world who surf the Internet. He is unusual in that he has compared the Internet to God. Writing in the magazine of the Church of England's Board of Social Responsibility, he said, 'It would seem that all the information in the world, all that is known, has been known, or might be needed to be known is available on the Internet. The human understanding of God is that he is all-knowing, all-powerful. So is the Internet God? Is it a reflection of the word of God? Is it a glimpse into the awesome nature of God?'

The Internet also offers a fast-track route to ordination. In the United States, the Rev. Daniel Zimmerman is offering ordination in his Universal Life Church on the World Wide Web for the incredible bargain price of just $7. This will empower you to absolve your own sins as well as other people's in the name of 'whatever your belief system dictates'. But that's not all. If you manage to persuade fifteen more people to sign up on the Church's 'chapel' – otherwise known as its web site – you will be canonised as a 'saint'!

Source: Adapted from The Times, 20 January 1998; The Church of England Newspaper, 27 March 1998.

Bible references: Job 36:22–26,37–41; Psalm 147:5; Isaiah 40:13–31; Romans 11:33–36; 1 Corinthians 2:9–16; 1 Timothy 3:1–13; Titus 1:6–9.

173. JARGON (Church, Communication, the Cross, Gifts of the Spirit, Jesus, Love, Romance, Sociology, Tongues, Humour)

At a conference of sociologists in America in 1977, love was defined as 'the cognitive-affective state characterised by intrusive and obsessive fantasising concerning reciprocity of amorant feelings by the object of the amorance'.

According to Bruce Reed in *The Dynamics of Religion*, the task of the local church is 'to monitor the oscillation process by containing or rendering manageable anxieties associated with the activities of the profane world so that individuals and institutions are able to carry out the tasks on which the survival and wellbeing of their social groups depends'.

For those who have ever wondered what the gift of tongues is, one author has written, in all seriousness: 'I want to propose that glossolalia should be defined as a vocalisation pattern, a speech automatism, that is produced on the substratum of hyperarousal dissociation, reflecting directly, in its segmental and suprasegmental structure, neurophysiologic processes present in this mental state.'

And finally, 'the person of Jesus, and especially his death on a cross', is explained by the authors of a book on postmodernism as 'a symbol of the counterideological intent of the biblical metanarrative and the paradigm or model of ethical human action, even in the face of massive injustice'. It's funny that they clarify the term 'paradigm', but leave the rest.

Source: Quoted in Bill Bryson, Mother Tongue: The English Language (Penguin, 1990), p 9; Bruce Reed quoted in Michael Green, The Peterborough Book (Sphere, 1982), pp 64–65; Felicitas D. Goodman, quoted in D.A. Carson, Showing the Spirit (Baker Book House, 1987), p 184; J. Richard Middleton and Brian J. Walsh, Truth is Stranger than it Used to Be (SPCK, 1995), p 105.

Bible references: Matthew 28:18–20; Acts 10:46; 19:6; Romans 3:25–26; 5:8; 12:9–13; 1 Corinthians 12:10,28,30; 13; 14:5–6,18, 21–23,39; 2 Corinthians 5:21; Galatians 3:13; 1 Peter 2:24; 1 John 3:16; 4:7–12.

174. MEDICINE (Alternative medicine, Doctors, Health, Herbalism, History, Paganism, Prayer, Science, Secularism, Superstition, Humour)

'I have an earache… '

2000 BC	'Here, eat this root.'
AD 1000	'That root is heathen. Here, say this prayer.'
AD 1850	'That prayer is superstition. Here, drink this potion.'
AD 1940	'That potion is snake oil. Here, swallow this pill.'
AD 1985	'That pill is ineffective. Here, take this antibiotic.'
AD 2000	'That antibiotic is unnatural. Here, eat this root.'

Source: New Scientist, September 1997, quoted in The Chichester Magazine, Spring 1998.

Bible references: Ecclesiastes 1:9–11; 3:15.

175. MIRACLES (Alcohol, Bible, Bureaucracy, Disability, Fish, Healing, Jesus, New Testament, Raising the dead, Walking on water, Humour)

If Jesus were alive today, he wouldn't be allowed to get away with half the miracles he performed. It's not just that we live in such a sceptical, rationalist age. It's all the red tape as well. Here are a few examples.

Turning water into wine
This would provoke immediate protests from the drinks industry, who would argue that it was unfair competition, amounting to a monopoly. It would also be denounced by various Christian bodies as irresponsible and likely to lead to drunkenness.

Feeding the multitude
Serving bread and fish to thousands of people at an outdoor event would require the approval of government health inspectors, to ensure that the food had been prepared by qualified food handlers in a hygienic environment. Baskets of leftovers would also need to be disposed of properly.

Walking on water
This could only be done if it was preceded by a disclaimer that nobody should try this at home, particularly not children or young people.

The miraculous catch of fish
Fish stocks are now rigorously conserved to protect against overfishing, and such large catches would undoubtedly exceed the fishermen's quotas, leading to stiff penalties.

Healing a man born blind

This apparent act of kindness would lead to all sorts of problems with the government benefits agency. All disability benefit would immediately be stopped, and the man in question would probably face an investigation into whether his previous claims had been genuine.

Raising the dead

Environmental health officers wouldn't be happy about this one, as there are stringent rules governing the proper disposal of bodies. There would also be major difficulties when the recently deceased tried to use their credit cards.

Source: Adapted from David Walters in Renewal, April 1999.

Bible references: Matthew 9:18–25; 14:13–21,23–33; 15:32–38; Mark 5:22–43; 6:32–44,47–51; 8:1–9; Luke 5:1–11; 7:11–15; 8:41–56; 9:10–17; John 2:1–11; 6:1–13,17–21; 9:1–7; 11:1–44; 21:1–14.

176. POSTMODERNISM (Despair, the Human condition, Individualism, Life, Loneliness, Pessimism)

John Dominic Crossan, hailed by many as a brilliant New Testament scholar, offers a profoundly pessimistic view of the human condition in the postmodern era: 'There is no lighthouse keeper. There is no lighthouse. There is no dry land. There are only people living on rafts made from their own imaginations. And there is the sea.'

Source: John Dominic Crossan, The Dark Interval: Towards a Theology of Story, p 44, quoted in J. Richard Middleton and Brian J. Walsh, Truth is Stranger than it Used to Be (SPCK, 1995), p 62.

Bible references: Psalms 10:4; 14:1–4; 53:1–4; Jeremiah 2:31; Romans 1:21,28; Revelation 3:17–18.

177. PRAYER (Idols, Intercession, Miracles, New Age, Royalty, Saints, Weather)

In June 1998, the summer after the death of Diana, Princess of Wales, an open-air concert was held in aid of the Princess Diana Memorial Fund at Althorp, her family home. It was a wet morning, but the rain stopped before the concert began. Later David Hasselhoff, an American TV actor who stars in the beach drama *Baywatch*, said that the change in the weather was due to the princess's intervention. He said that he had prayed, 'Diana, if you can do this one last thing, part the skies.' 'And she did,' he added. 'It was the most amazing thing she did today.'

Source: Adapted from The Daily Telegraph, 29 June 1998.

Bible references: Deuteronomy 3:24; 4:39; Isaiah 44:6–8; 1 Corinthians 8:4–6.

178. TECHNOLOGY (Computers, Idols, Other faiths, Science, Worship)

An article in the *New York Times* in December 1990 told how a group of fifty Japanese engineers held a religious ceremony at a Buddhist temple to pay their respects to old computer chips. The chief priest, dressed in purple robes, bowed low and chanted as a large tray covered in used parts was placed before a statue of the Buddha, waiting to be taken up to heaven. The priest, Shogen Kobayashi, said that he had 'no doubt that revering the chip will pay off for the Japanese people'. As well as performing these annual ceremonies, the engineers said that in time they intended to put up a monument to these loyal but now defunct computer components.

Source: Adapted from Russell Chandler, Racing Towards 2001 (HarperCollins, Zondervan, 1992), p 308.

Bible references: Psalms 115:4–8; 135:15–18; Isaiah 44:9–20; 46:6–7; Jeremiah 2:27–28; 10:1–16; 16:19–20; Habakkuk 2:18–19; Acts 17:22–31; Romans 1:22–23,25; 1 Corinthians 8:4–6.

179. WOMEN (Cosmetics, Counselling, Culture, Human nature, Magazines, Media, Money, Morality, Relationships, Secularism, Sex)

In 1997 the Social Affairs Unit examined eleven different magazines with a combined readership of 3.7 million women, including *Cosmopolitan, Elle,* and *Company*. Then they drew up a composite picture of the image of today's typical woman based on what they had read.

> Today's British woman has no children, no cares, and no responsibilities. Her life is a round of indulgences of a distinctly tawdry kind. She rarely thinks, and when she does it is about sex. In pursuit of sex and other whims she is happy to desert a faithful and loving husband. Increasingly, she enjoys drunken pranks once associated with adolescent boys. She calls this 'GIRL POWER'. When sex and exhibitionism pall she soaks up the make-believe world of soap opera as if it were real. Her world is devoid of values except those of fashion. She rarely needs to make judgements so long as she is wearing this season's lipstick and the current partner has an ample bank balance. She is committed only to her favourite film star's choice of underwear, indifferent to literature, art, learning and civic responsibility and reluctant to make an effort in any cause except the gym. When these narcissistic and trivial attitudes occasionally cause problems,

there is always the counsellor to turn to and the latest therapy to make her feel good about herself again.

Source: Digby Anderson and Michael Mosbacher, 'The British Woman Today', quoted in The Church of England Newspaper, 28 November 1997.

Bible references: Proverbs 31:10–31; Romans 12:2; 1 Timothy 2:9–10; Titus 2:3–5; 1 Peter 3:3–4.

MONEY, MONEY, MONEY

180. EXCUSES (Confession, Crime, Cults, Gullibility, Judgement, Robbery, Sin, Stealing, Humour)

In May 1998 Russell Grant-McVicar was jailed for fifteen years for a series of armed bank raids. That's not so unusual, but what was remarkable was the defence that Grant-McVicar offered. He admitted that he had committed the sixteen robbery, escape and firearms offences that he was charged with, but pleaded not guilty because, he claimed, he was acting on the orders of what he described as 'the most powerful cult on the planet'. They had threatened to kill him and his daughter, he said, unless he carried out the robberies 'as a spiritual statement', to draw attention to the suffering of starving children in the Third World. He was then asked how it was that if this was true, he had spent the proceeds of the robberies on himself. He explained that the cult had not actually asked him to hand over the £100,000 that he'd stolen, either to them or to the starving children, so he had assumed that he could keep it.

Source: Adapted from The Daily Telegraph, 23 May 1998.

Bible references: 1 John 1:8.

181. FORGERY (Church, Clergy, Collection, Crime, Excuses, Generosity, Giving, Offertory, Humour)

In 1979 police in Rome caught a forty-nine-year-old parish priest, Father Guido Antonelli, producing forged 50,000 lire notes on a printing press in his church. The priest told them that he had been forced to turn to crime because his congregation weren't putting enough in the offertory.

Source: Adapted from Bill Bryson, Bizarre World (Warner Books, 1995), p 131.

Bible references: Malachi 3:8–10; Romans 2:21–23.

182. GIVING (Church, Churchgoing, Collection, Gambling, Lottery, Offertory, Prize draw, Raffle, Wealth, Humour)

At the Sweet Heaven Holy Church of God in Carrollton, Virginia, they've come up with a novel way of attracting people to come to church and give. Everyone who puts money into the collection plate receives a ticket with a number on it. At the end of the service there is a prize draw, and the person holding the lucky number is given $100 from the offering. It wasn't reported what happens if the total offering comes to less than $100!

Source: Adapted from The Church of England Newspaper, 1996.

Bible references: 2 Corinthians 9:6–11.

183. GIVING (Church, Collection, Generosity, Offertory, Shopping, Spending, Wealth, Humour)

It was Monday morning in the bank, and a fifty pound note and a pound coin happened to get into conversation. 'Had a good weekend?' asked the pound. 'Oh, yes,' the bank note answered. 'I had a wonderful time. I had a lie-in in the wallet on Saturday morning, went to a designer dress shop in the afternoon, an expensive restaurant on Saturday evening, and then a health club on Sunday. What about you?'

'Oh, the usual,' said the pound coin. 'Round a load of shops on Saturday, then church on Sunday morning. Don't you ever go to church?'

'You must be joking!' sniffed the fifty pound note. 'No one would ever put *me* in a church collection!'

Source: Adapted from Keith Tondeur, What Jesus Said about Money and Possessions, reproduced in Renewal, December 1998.

Bible references: Proverbs 3:9–10; 11:24–25; 22:9; Malachi 3:8–10; Mark 4:24–25; Luke 6:38; 1 Corinthians 16:1–2; 2 Corinthians 8:3–4; 9:6–15.

184. GIVING (Church, Clergy, Collection, Generosity, Offertory, Humour)

The veteran newspaper writer Bill Deedes once reported that at Ian Paisley's church in Belfast the collection was taken up not in little bags but in buckets. When people had given their contributions and the buckets were taken forward, Paisley would look in the buckets and see how much was in them. Then he would often declare, 'The Lord is not satisfied!' and the buckets would be sent round again until the Lord – or the minister at least – was satisfied.

Source: Adapted from The Daily Telegraph, 17 February 1996.

Bible references: Proverbs 3:9–10; 11:24–25; 22:9; Malachi 3:8–10; Mark 4:24–25; 12:41–44; Luke 6:38; 21:1–4; 1 Corinthians 16:1–2; 2 Corinthians 8:12; 9:6–15.

185. HAPPINESS (Depression, Dissatisfaction, Life, Loneliness, Materialism, Modern life, Psychology, Wealth)

Money doesn't buy you happiness, and if proof were needed, psychologist Oliver James revealed in a book published in 1997 that modern men and women are more depressed than any previous generation. Rates of clinical depression are ten times higher among people born since the Second World War than among those born before World War I, with women born after 1960 being most at risk. Modern life seems less and less able to meet our expectations. James says, 'It makes us feel like losers, even if we are winners.'

Times columnist Simon Jenkins commented:

> A generation that is the most comfortable in history is also the most depressed. The new anguish of middle-class Britain (and Europe and America) is a realisation that conventional 'success' is worse than being no road to happiness. It can so depress the serotonin levels in the brain as to be a direct path to misery. As James ranges from one case history to another, we are left with a bleak conclusion. The 1960s were right. The fragmenting of communities, the pressure of free-market employment, the incentive to short-term material gratification have indeed led to loneliness and depression. The more we expect of prosperity, the less it seems able to deliver.

Source: Adapted from The Times, 3 September 1997.

Bible references: Ecclesiastes 2:1–11; 5:10–19; Matthew 6:19–34; 16:26; Mark 8:36–37; Luke 12:15–34; 1 Timothy 6:6–10,17–19.

186. HONESTY (Commandments, Crime, Dishonesty, Hypocrisy, Morality, Stealing, Humour)

Two women happened to meet on a bus, and one confessed to her friend, 'You know, I'm a bit ashamed about this, but I managed to get on without paying the fare.' Her friend replied, 'Oh you shouldn't feel bad about that, everybody does it. But mind you, honesty *does* pay. I paid my fare with a five-pound note, and the driver gave me change for a tenner!'

Source: Adapted from William L. Self and Caroline Shealy Self, Confessions of a Nomad (Peachtree Publishers, 1983), p 101.

Bible references: Luke 16:8–13.

187. THE LOTTERY (Contentment, Envy, Families, Happiness, Human nature, Life, Luck, Ownership, Possessions, Satisfaction, Wealth, Work)

Every week millions of people buy their lottery tickets with the dream of becoming a millionaire. In January 1996 that's just what happened to a hospital orderly called John McGuiness, who won £10 million on the National Lottery. Before that he'd been earning just £150 a week; now he can afford to buy anything he wants. So he spent a million pounds on a house – a mansion to be more accurate – over a million pounds on cars, three quarters of a million on jewellery for his girlfriend, half a million on holidays, and has given £1.3m to his local football club. But because of the interest he's earning, he's still got almost £10 million in the bank.

Yet the remarkable thing is that John says that the money has not made him any happier at all. 'It hasn't brought me any real contentment,' he says. 'I'm no happier since I won the Lottery. The only time I really got a buzz was the night I won. Then everything started to come down bit by bit. When I buy something new it does give me a fifteen-second buzz. But it's a high that doesn't last. A house is just a house and a car is just a heap of metal. When I was working at least I felt as though I was achieving something. I know £10 million is a lot of money, but if I'd stayed as I was I'd be just as happy.'

And in one area of John's life the win has actually made things worse. Although he's given a lot of money to his family, it has only caused problems. 'The money has caused so much hassle within the family,' he says. 'No matter how much you give them it's still not enough. We were a very close family before the lottery, but the money has caused a lot of heartache, and in the backs of our minds we know something has gone. A gulf has opened up.'

Source: Adapted from The Sunday Mirror, 31 January 1999.

Bible references: Proverbs 30:8–9; Ecclesiastes 2:1–11; 5:10–19; Matthew 6:19–21; 16:26; Mark 8:36–37; Luke 12:15–34; 1 Timothy 6:6–10, 17–19; Revelation 3:17.

188. POSSESSIONS (Discipleship, Freedom, Hardship, Ownership, Persecution, Presence of God, Priorities, Prison, Security, Suffering, Wealth)

The poet Irina Ratushinskaya spent many years in a Russian labour camp. Now free and living in the West, she reflected:

> A person who is deprived of everything, of family, of contact with friends, who is totally isolated, alone, without any property at all, not even a toothbrush, has nothing left to lose. An enormous, powerful sense of security follows. Instead of panic, one feels God's hand on one's shoulder. We all felt that nothing really bad could happen to us: we all thought, 'If they kill us today, tomorrow we will be in heaven.'
>
> I wish I had the same feeling now, but I don't. Under such pressure, God feels really close: it's easier to serve God when in trouble than on holiday. When I came to the West, I thought, 'Now I'm in a world of holidaymakers.'
>
> When Jesus came, he said, 'Leave everything you have.' That was a frightening demand. A person can only develop if he or she is able to let go. It was easier for us to take risks back in the Russian labour camps because we had nothing to lose. Now, after spending ten years in the West, I do have something to lose.

Source: Renewal, January 1998.

Bible references: Deuteronomy 8:12–14; Matthew 6:19–21; 19:21–29; Mark 10:21–30; Luke 12:33–34; 14:33; 18:22–30; Acts 2:44–45; 4:32–35; Philippians 4:11–13; 1 Timothy 6:17–19; Hebrews 10:34.

189. SATISFACTION (Friendship, Happiness, Health, Human nature, Life, Love, Ownership, Possessions, Wealth)

Money can buy you a house, but it can't buy you a home.
Money can buy you insurance, but it can't buy you security.
Money can buy you entertainment, but it can't buy you happiness.
Money can buy you medicine, but it can't buy you health.
Money can buy you a bed, but it can't buy you sleep.
Money can buy you companionship, but it can't buy you friendship.
Money can buy you sex, but it can't buy you love.

Source: Adapted from J. John, God's Top Ten (Kingsway, 1995), p 20.

Bible references: Ecclesiastes 2:1–11; 5:10–19; Matthew 6:19–34; Luke 12:15–34; 1 Timothy 6:6–10,17–19.

190. WEALTH (Death, Envy, Fame, Funerals, Life, Lifestyle, Ownership, Possessions, Humour)

The story is told of a very wealthy American who left instructions in his will that he wanted to be sent off in unforgettable style. He laid down that he should be buried in his gold-plated Cadillac, propped up behind the steering wheel, his pockets full of cash and an expensive cigar in his hand. The TV cameras whirred as the car was lowered into the enormous grave, and one onlooker was heard to say to his neighbour, 'Boy, that guy sure knew how to live!'

Source: Adapted from Calvin Miller, The Empowered Leader (Broadman and Holman, 1995), p 30.

Bible references: Job 31:24–28; Psalm 49; Proverbs 11:4,28; Ecclesiastes 5:10–19; Matthew 16:26; Mark 8:36–37; Luke 12:13–21; 1 Timothy 6:6–10,17–19.

191. WEALTH (Envy, Fame, Humiliation, Influence, Life, Power, Security, Suicide)

In 1923, nine of the richest men in America met at Chicago's Edgewater Beach Hotel. Their wealth and influence made them among the most powerful men in the nation. They were: the president of the New York Stock Exchange, the most influential financier on Wall Street, the head of the world's biggest monopoly, the presidents of America's biggest steel corporation, electricity company, and gas company, a powerful wheat baron, the president of an international bank, and the Secretary of the Interior.

Such men would have been the envy of America at the time, but just twenty-five years later the picture was dramatically different. By 1948 one of the men was insane, two had recently been released from prison, three others were bankrupt, and the remaining three had all committed suicide.

Source: Adapted from Sermons Illustrated 8.1989.22.

Bible references: Job 31:24–28; Psalm 49; Proverbs 11:4,28; 18:11–12; 23:5; Ecclesiastes 5:10–19; Jeremiah 9:23–24; Matthew 6:19–21; 16:26; 19:21; Mark 8:36–37; Luke 1:51–53; 6:24–25; 12:13–21; 18:22; 1 Timothy 6:6–10,17–19; Hebrews 10:34; 11:26.

192. WEALTH (Inequality, Influence, Poverty, Power, Social action)

In 1998 a UN report revealed that the three richest people in the world had more money between them than the forty-eight poorest countries all put together. The three were all Americans: Bill Gates of the Microsoft computer corporation, Helen Walton, whose family owned the Wal-Mart store chain, and Warren Buffett, an investor. According to the report, Bill Gates alone could pay for everybody in the world to have a basic education, access to health care, decent sanitation and safe drinking water, and still have $18 billion left over.

If the list were extended, and the world's 225 richest people were to pool their money, they would between them have over $1 trillion, which is roughly equal to the combined annual income of 47% of the entire world population, about 2.5 billion people.

Nor is it only at the highest level that there is this glaring inequality. The report estimated that every child born in America, Britain or France would in the course of his or her lifetime consume, waste or pollute more than fifty times the amount of a child from a developing country. But at the same time it would be those born in developing countries who would suffer the most from environmental damage, because they would be more likely to burn traditional fuels, use leaded petrol and live near factories or rubbish dumps. As a UN administrator said, 'Not everyone has been invited to the party.'

Source: Adapted from The Daily Telegraph, 10 September 1998.

Bible references: Job 31:24–28; Psalms 49; 52:7; 62:8–9; Proverbs 10:15; 11:23–28; 22:22–23; Jeremiah 9:23–24; Matthew 16:26; Mark 8:36–37; 10:23–25; Luke 12:13–21; 1 Timothy 6:6–10,17–19.

MISTAKES AND MISUNDERSTANDINGS

193. BEGINNINGS (Art, Poison, Potential, Humour)

The painter Edouard Manet is now recognised as one of the great masters of Impressionist art, but his career didn't get off to a very promising start. His first 'commission' was as a sixteen-year-old sailor visiting Rio de Janeiro. The ship's cargo of cheeses had deteriorated during the long sea voyage, and Manet was asked to touch up the rinds, which had been damaged on the journey. Unfortunately the paint which he used had lead in it, and the cheeses caused a local outbreak of lead poisoning.

Source: Adapted from Patricia Wright, Eyewitness Art: Manet (Dorling Kindersley, 1993), p 7.

Bible references: 1 Samuel 17:17; Psalm 25:7.

194. BIBLE (Filofax, Juries, Law courts, Modern life, Humour)

Many people couldn't live without their filofax. Many clergy couldn't live without their filofax. But few of them have made the same mistake as the young man who mistook his filofax for a Bible. It happened at the

Old Bailey in 1989, when the jury was being sworn in for a rape case. One of the twelve jurors was about to swear the oath on his filofax when a court usher noticed the mistake and handed him a Bible instead.

Source: Adapted from The Daily Telegraph, 5 July 1989.

Bible references: 2 Timothy 2:15; 3:15–17; Hebrews 4:12.

195. DISCERNMENT (Arrogance, Authority, Casinos, Gambling, Judgement, Poker, Pride, Humour)

At the Mirage Hotel in Las Vegas, a security guard was told to collect the winnings from a poker game. He pushed his way to the table, ignoring the fact that the hand he was interrupting was worth £40,000. He was simply doing his job, so he was distinctly unimpressed when he felt a hand on his shoulder, and a voice told him to 'scram'.

'Who the hell are you?' he asked.

'I'm Bobby Baldwin,' the man answered. 'Senior Executive President of the casino.'

'If you're president of this casino, I'm Adolf Hitler,' the guard replied, grabbing the man and pushing him against the wall. It was only when he tried to force Mr Baldwin to leave the casino that he discovered his mistake. He did not subsequently remain on the pay roll.

Source: Adapted from The Daily Telegraph, 16 December 1995.

Bible references: Exodus 22:28; Proverbs 16:18; Ecclesiastes 10:20; Acts 23:1–5; Romans 13:1–7; Titus 3:1–2; 1 Peter 2:17.

196. DISCERNMENT (Judgement, Misinterpretation, Repentance, Sin, Humour)

Sometimes we fail to take seriously things in our lives that need to get sorted out and put right. A ten-year-old girl in southern Sweden went to the doctor with a pain in her thigh. She had been playing outside her home when she suddenly felt a pain in her leg. She looked down and saw an insect crawling out of her jeans, so naturally she assumed she'd been bitten or stung. The problem was that the bite, or sting, or whatever it was, just didn't respond to treatment. It was only after six weeks that the doctors discovered why: the girl had a .22 rifle bullet lodged in her thigh. After the bullet had been removed, she soon recovered.

Source: Adapted from The Daily Telegraph, 9 August 1997.

Bible references: Matthew 9:10–13; Mark 2:15–17; Luke 5:30–32; 7:29–30; John 9:39–41; 1 Corinthians 5:1–5; 2 Corinthians 4:3–4; 12:20–21; Revelation 3:17–19.

197. HOLIDAYS (Hospitality, Hotels, Language, Misinterpretation, Translation, Humour)

The broadcaster Cliff Michelmore collected a number of quotations from foreign holiday brochures:

- If this is your first visit to our hotel you are welcome to it.
- You will not be likely to forget quickly your experience with us.
- Situated in the shadiest part of the town, you cannot fail to remark from the window the odours of the pine trees and our swimming pool.

- If you wish for breakfast, lift the telephone, ask for room service, and this will be enough for you to bring your food up.
- On gala nights the chef throws his best dishes, and all water used in cooking has been passed by the manager personally.
- If your wife needs something to do, she should apply to our suggestive head porter, but all our staff are courteous, and to ladies too attentive.
- We would very much like to have relations with you, and we will be most happy to dispose of all your clients.

Source: Quoted in Pass the Port (Christian Brann, 1976), pp 175–176.

198. INTERPRETATION (Archaeology, Early church, History, Rome, Saints, Humour)

In 1802 during excavations near Rome three tiles were dug up bearing the inscriptions 'PAX TE', 'CUM FI', and 'LUMENA', not far from some bones and a jug containing a darkish residue. The tiles were put together to read, 'Pax tecum Filumena', that is to say, 'Peace be with you, Philomena' and it was presumed that Philomena was the young woman whose bones lay nearby. Having put these two pieces of the jigsaw together, it was then deduced that the dried liquid in the jug was Philomena's blood, which in turn led to the inescapable concusion that this was the shrine of a hitherto unknown saint, an early Christian virgin martyr.

One hundred and fifty years later, in 1961, an American bishop was on the point of dedicating a new church to Saint Philomena when word came from the Vatican that they had had second thoughts. The tiles were probably not originally connected with the bones or the jug, and could more plausibly be reassembled in a different order and translated: 'Light and peace to you, with faith.' The cult of St Philomena was abolished with immediate effect. The American bishop dedicated his church to the Precious Blood instead.

Source: Adapted from Gavin White, The Mother Church Your Mother Never Told You Of (SCM, 1993), p 7.

199. LANGUAGE (Army, Authority, Judgement, Military service, Misunderstanding, Humour)

The story is told of an immigrant who enlisted in the US Army. His one big problem was his English – he still wasn't very good at it. One day the troops were told that the general was going to inspect them in a few days' time, and that he might well talk to them individually and ask them questions about themselves. The men in this particular soldier's unit realised that he was going to be in big trouble unless they gave him some help, so they decided he needed some coaching beforehand.

'Now listen,' they said to him, 'The general always asks the same questions, so you just need to learn the answers off by heart. The first thing he asks is, "How many years have you been in the army?", so you answer, "Two, sir." The second thing he asks is, "And how old are you?" so you say, "Twenty-two, sir." Then the last question is always, "Have you been getting good food and good training?" You answer, "Both, sir." Two, twenty-two and both. Just remember those. OK?'

The man worked hard to learn his answers until the day of the inspection came. As the general walked down the lines, he stopped from time to time in front of particular soldiers and asked them a few questions. Sure enough, they were the same questions that he always asked. The only trouble was, he sometimes varied the order he asked them in. So he stopped in front of the soldier in question and said, 'How old are you, soldier?' 'Two, sir.' 'Two?' repeated the general, 'And how many years have you been in the army?' 'Twenty-two, sir,' the soldier answered. 'What do you take me for, man?' the general asked angrily, 'An idiot or a fool?' 'Both, sir,' the soldier replied.

Source: Adapted from Larry Moyer, in Haddon Robinson, ed., Biblical Sermons (Baker Book House, 1989), pp 203–204.

Bible references: Exodus 22:28; Ecclesiastes 10:20; Acts 23:1–5; Romans 13:1–7; Titus 3:1–2; 1 Peter 2:17.

200. PLANNING (Diving, Experience, Frustration, Preparedness, Humour)

In 1979 the members of a scuba diving team from Cornwall decided to go diving in a Scottish lake, Loch Buidhe. They got permission from the loch's owner, loaded up all their equipment, and drove the 700 miles to Scotland. They unloaded all their diving gear and lugged it 3,000 feet up a mountain to reach the loch. It was only then that they discovered their mistake. Loch Buidhe is only six inches deep!

Source: Adapted from Bill Bryson, Bizarre World (Warner Books, 1995), p 44.

Bible references: Proverbs 15:22; 16:9; 19:21; Luke 14:28–33.

201. PLANNING (Children, Drugs, Experience, Humour)

It was one of those things that seemed like a great idea at the time: send to children in primary schools free pencils with the slogan 'Too Cool To Do Drugs' printed on them. Anti-drugs campaigners sent out hundreds of these pencils across New York state before teachers discovered the problem with them. After the children had sharpened their pencils a few times, the message read, 'Cool To Do Drugs'. After a few more sharpenings, they got down to simply, 'Do Drugs'. At that point the Bureau for At-Risk Youth, whose bright idea it was, decided not to give out any more of the pencils.

Source: Adapted from The Daily Telegraph, 12 December 1998.

Bible references: Proverbs 15:22; 16:9; 19:21; Luke 14:28–33.

202. PREDICTION (Cars, Discernment, Faith, Inventions, Newspapers, Potential, Prophecy, Science, Telephone, Television, Vision)

In August 1946, Lieutenant-Colonel C.P. Boas was an officer with the British forces occupying Germany when he came across a car production plant in a place called Wolfsburg. He thought that the car that was being made there had real potential, and wrote to the Board of Trade urging them to buy the factory. This, he wrote, 'would not only satisfy the low price demand of the domestic motor user but be an extremely attractive proposition for overseas markets'. The Board of Trade duly sent a group of civil servants and motor manufacturers over to Germany to look at the car, which was known as the Kdf-Wagen, but decided against taking it any further. 'It is not considered to have a long-term civilian application,' they wrote. And so Volkswagen went on to produce and sell some 20 million Beetles, but without any profit to the British government.

Sir Ernest Rutherford, though a great scientist, showed a similar lack of foresight. He was the head of the Cavendish laboratories in Cambridge, where in May 1932 John Cockcroft and Ernest Walton managed to split the atom using the world's first successful particle accelerator. Although Rutherford was himself a pioneer in the field of atomic particle physics, he declared that anyone who believed that this could be a source of power was 'talking moonshine'.

Similarly, when Alexander Graham Bell and his assistant Thomas Watson demonstrated their new invention, the telephone, to Western Union in 1876, the company's executives wrote back, 'Mr Bell, after careful consideration of your invention, while it is a very interesting novelty, we have come to the conclusion that it has no commercial possibilities.' They added that they saw no future for what was, in effect, no more than 'an electrical toy'.

The New York Times showed itself to be equally bad at predicting the future in 1939, when large crowds were drawn by a demonstration of television at the World's Fair in New York. The paper stated that television would never be a serious rival to radio because 'people must sit and keep their eyes glued on a screen; the average American family hasn't time for it'. If only they knew!

Source: Adapted from The Telegraph magazine, 15 and 22 November 1997; Bill Bryson, Made in America (Minerva, 1995), pp 113, 270.

Bible references: 2 Chronicles 24:19; Proverbs 19:2; Jeremiah 7:24–28; 25:3–7; 26:4–6; Hosea 4:5–6.

203. SCIENCE (Arrogance, Astronomy, Human nature, Knowledge, Pride, Truth, Humour)

Science is by its very nature provisional, as this comment by David Wilkinson, a fellow of the Royal Astronomical Society, underlines. 'The great British astronomer Sir Arthur Eddington once stated that there were 15,747, 724,136,275,002,577,605,653,961,181,555,468,044, 717,914,527,116,709,366,231,425,076,185,631,031,296 protons in the universe and the same number of electrons. He was wrong!'

Source: David Wilkinson and Rob Frost, Thinking Clearly About God and Science (Monarch, 1996), p 64.

Bible references: Genesis 15:5; Job 9:1–12; 38; Psalms 8; 144:3–4; Proverbs 16:18; Isaiah 40:12–20; Romans 1:19–20.

204. SCIENCE (Alcohol, Biology, Chemistry, Children, Deacons, First aid, Fossils, Medicine, Misunderstanding, the Moon, the Pope, School, Teachers, Humour)

A teacher in the United States compiled the following list of scientific insights from test papers and essays written by students at school and college.

- Water is composed of two gins, oxygin and hydrogin. Oxygin is pure gin. Hydrogin is gin and water.
- H_2O is hot water, and CO_2 is cold water.
- To collect fumes of sulphur, hold a deacon over a test tube.
- Dew is formed on leaves when the sun shines down on them and makes them perspire.
- A super saturated solution is one that holds more than it can hold.

- Mushrooms always grow in damp places and so they look like umbrellas.
- The tides are a fight between the earth and moon. All water tends towards the moon, because there is no water in the moon and nature abhors a vacuum. I forget where the sun joins in this fight.
- The moon is a planet just like the earth, only it is even deader.
- A fossil is an extinct animal. The older it is, the more extinct it is.
- The skeleton is what is left after the insides have been taken out and the outsides have been taken off. The purpose of the skeleton is something to hitch meat to.

Some definitions:
- Germinate: to become a naturalised German.
- Litre: a nest of young puppies.
- Magnet: something you find crawling all over a dead cat.
- Momentum: what you give a person when they are going away.
- Rhubarb: a kind of celery gone bloodshot.
- Vacuum: a large, empty space where the Pope lives.

Some helpful advice:
- To remove dust from the eye, pull the eye down over the nose.
- For a nosebleed: put the nose much lower than the body until the heart stops.
- For a dog bite: put the dog away for several days. If he has not recovered, then kill it.
- For a head cold: use an agoniser to spray the nose until it drops in your throat.
- To keep milk from turning sour: keep it in the cow.

Source: Terry Williams and Esther Bailey of Scripture Union.

205. SIGNS (Interpretation, Misinterpretation, Misunderstanding, Humour)

Wiltshire police were alarmed to come across a coachload of Japanese tourists standing in the middle of the A303, which is a very busy road, taking photographs of Stonehenge. They didn't seem to be worried by the cars and lorries whizzing past them on both sides. It was only when the police officers had shepherded the party off the road and onto the safety of the verge that they discovered the reason why the tourists had thought they were safe. Pointing to a speed camera sign by the side of the road, they explained that they had assumed that this was a designated photography area.

Source: Adapted from The Daily Telegraph, 27 September 1997.

Bible references: Matthew 16:1–4,5–12; Mark 8:14–21; Luke 15:54–56.

206. TRANSLATION (Interpretation, Language, Misinterpretation, Misunderstanding, Humour)

Trying to speak another language is fraught with difficulties, and even the professionals sometimes get it wrong. There was, for example, a translator at a European summit who thought that Mrs Thatcher was talking about 'throwing a Spaniard in the works', and a French interpreter at a discussion on artificial insemination who innocently translated 'frozen semen' as 'matelots congelés'. It's a lot more understandable when politicians get it wrong. One of the more unfortunate gaffes was reportedly made by President Roosevelt during a radio broadcast to Morocco during the Second World War. What he meant to say was, 'I love your farms, I love your towns': 'J'aime vos fermes,

MADE IN AMERICA

207. AMAZING DISCOVERIES (Archaeology, Bible, Creation, Eden, Gullibility, Media, Newspapers, Old Testament, Tabloids, Humour)

In February 1997 the American tabloid *Weekly World News* splashed over its front page the eye-catching headline, 'Shocking Bible Secret REVEALED! ADAM AND EVE HAD A BABY GIRL! Tiny skeleton rests amid ancient bones in Adam and Eve's grave!' This was next to a photograph of two adult skeletons, one of them cradling the skeleton of an infant.

Inside, the paper repeats its earlier report – unnoticed by many – that in 1992 archaeologist Dr Jonathan Richard had stunned the world when he revealed that he had discovered the bones of Adam and Eve forty miles south of Denver in Colorado. The proof that these truly were the bodies of our first ancestors was supposedly provided by the fact that 'the male skeleton was missing a rib – and that rib was found grafted to the female's spine'. Now, five years later, Dr Richard had decided that the world was ready for his next amazing discovery – Adam and Eve's baby daughter, aged about three weeks.

The paper then quotes the Rev. Deke Smollins, whom it describes as an 'Australian minister and Bible authority', as saying

> If this discovery is genuine – and it certainly appears to be – we now have concrete proof that Adam and Eve gave birth to a daughter. That means all their children are not mentioned in the Bible. This should silence the cynics who say the Bible is false because Cain couldn't have found a wife. If this daughter was not mentioned, then there could well have been other daughters. And if there were, Cain could have married one of them.

The Rev. Smollins – the reputed Bible authority – seems surprisingly unfamiliar with Genesis 5:4, which explicitly says that Adam 'had other sons and daughters'. But the more interesting question which he and the paper failed to ask is how the bodies of Adam, Eve and the baby all came to be buried together (the skeletons are intertwined) in the same grave. That would mean that they had all died at the same time. Was this the first case of mass murder? Was Cain a serial killer? It surely can't be long before the paper makes the claim!

Source: Adapted from Weekly World News, 25 February 1997.

Bible references: Genesis 2:7–23; 4:1–2,17; 5:1–4.

208. THE BIBLE (Confectionery, Food, Lifestyle, Modern life, Sweets, Humour)

In the United States you can now buy the world's first Christian breath fresheners. Each mint has a cross stamped on it, and each packet of mints carries a Bible verse. Unfortunately it wasn't reported which Bible verses have been chosen. They presumably include Psalm 119:103, 'How sweet are your words to my taste, sweeter than honey to my mouth' (*with no added sugar!*). But probably not Job 20:12, 'Evil is sweet in his mouth, and he hides it under his tongue.'

Source: Adapted from Tear Times, Winter 1997.

Bible references: Job 20:12; Psalm 19:9–10; 119:103; Proverbs 16:24; Ezekiel 3:3; Revelation 10:9–10.

209. FAITH (Afterlife, Assurance, Boldness, Church, Confidence, Courage, Death, Heaven, Martyrdom, Opposition, Persecution, Violence, Witness, Youth)

In September 1999 a gunman entered a youth prayer meeting at the Wedgwood Baptist Church in Texas and shot dead seven people. Eyewitnesses said that Larry Gene Ashbrook was cursing Christians as he came into the church and started firing. At first some of the students thought it was a stunt, but as the bullets started flying the youth minister yelled, 'Get down, this is real!' and people dived for cover under the pews. But then one of the teenagers stood up and said to the gunman, 'Sir, I know what you need: you need Jesus Christ in your life.'

The gunman muttered something about why was the boy still standing up, to which the nineteen-year-old replied, 'I know where I'm going when I die; what about you?' There was a pause, and then the gunman sat down on the back pew and shot himself. The teenager wasn't hurt.

Source: Adapted from the Christian Herald, 25 September 1999.

Bible references: John 10:28–29; 11:25–27; Romans 1:16; 6:8–10; 8:11,18,35–39; 1 Corinthians 6:14; 2 Corinthians 4:13–14; 5:1; Colossians 4:5–6; 1 Thessalonians 4:13–18; 2 Timothy 1:8–9,12; 2:11–12; 4:17–18; 1 Peter 3:15–16; 1 John 3:1–2.

210. FAME (Animals, Cheese, Church, Fish, Insects, Pride, Records, Humour)

The cry of the citizens of Babel, 'Let's make a name for ourselves', has echoed down the ages. In America it seems as if every community wants to attract visitors by some claim to fame. In Hidalgo in Texas they've got a twenty-foot-long killer bee, made out of steel and fibreglass, to mark the fact that this was the spot where the aggressive African bee made its first reported appearance in the United States. But don't imagine that this is America's biggest insect. In Colorado Springs, Colorado, there is a thirty-five-foot model of a Hercules beetle, while the New England Pest Control Company in Providence, Rhode Island, have a blue termite on their roof fifty-eight feet long, with a forty-two foot wingspan.

Less frightening but equally spectacular is the world's largest fibreglass fish, a muskie five stories high and 145 feet long, housing the Freshwater Fishing Hall of Fame in Hayward, Wisconsin. New Salem, North Dakota, is the home of the world's biggest fibreglass cow, fifty feet long, thirty-eight feet high, and weighing six tons. But that's nothing in comparison with the world's largest concrete bull, in Audubon, Iowa, which measures fifteen feet from horn to horn and weighs in at a massive forty-five tons. For those who like to know such things, his name is Albert. Audubon also claims to be the home of the world's biggest coffee pot, holding no fewer than 600,000 cups.

An even more bizarre record is the world's largest ball of twine, which is to be found in Darwin, Minnesota. It weighs 17,400 lb and took one man forty-one years to make. Didn't he have anything better to do? And in Collinsville, Illinois, you can see what is believed to be the world's biggest ketchup bottle, seventy feet tall on a hundred-foot steel base. Sadly, the giant cheese in Berlin,

Ohio, which was claimed by locals to be the world's largest, is no more. In 1997 the refrigeration unit broke down and the whole thing went rotten.

The competition for the title of the holder of the world's largest chair has so far involved up to nine different towns. At present the champion seems to be Anniston in Alabama, whose chair stands thirty-three feet high, and is said to be able to withstand winds of up to eighty-five miles per hour. The citizens of Wingdale, New York, dismantled their twenty-five foot chair because young people 'were climbing up and doing unsafe things on it'.

There is equally keen competition for the title of the world's smallest church, with no fewer than ten contenders in nine different states. The winner appears to be the church in Wiscasset, Maine, which encloses just thirty square feet. For some bizarre reason it also has a large plastic golf ball impaled on its steeple.

Source: Adapted from The Daily Telegraph, 4 July 1998; The Sunday Times, 16 August 1998.

Bible references: Genesis 11:1–9; Psalm 49:11–13; Daniel 4:28–33.

211. INVOLVEMENT (Commitment, Reward, Service, Volunteers, Humour)

There was once a wealthy Texan who invited a group of guests round to his huge ranch for a party. As they are standing beside the swimming pool he points out to them that there's a shark swimming in it. Then he says, 'I'll give a million dollars or the hand of my beautiful daughter in marriage to the man who dares to swim one length of that pool.'

No sooner are the words out of his mouth when there's an almighty splash and there is a man in the pool, swimming with all his might towards the far end. He just makes it ahead of the shark, he hauls himself out of the water, and as he stands there, dripping wet, the Texan rushes up to congratulate him. 'Well, my friend,' he says, shaking him by the hand, 'Which will it be? Do you want the million dollars or the hand of my daughter?'

'All I want,' the man answered, 'is the name of the guy who pushed me in!'

Source: Unknown.

212. LAW (Fish, Food, Insects, Pharisees, Humour)

There are several bizarre local laws on the statute books in America:

- For instance, it's illegal to slurp your soup in a restaurant in New Jersey.
- In Oklahoma it's unlawful to get a fish drunk, or to try to catch whales in a river or lake.
- In Pennsylvania, cafés are not allowed to sell ring doughnuts, while in Massachusetts they are not permitted to serve coffee to babies.
- In Lexington, Kentucky, you cannot carry an ice-cream cone in your pocket.
- In Waterloo in Nebraska, barbers are prohibited from eating onions between seven o'clock in the morning and seven in the evening.
- Finally, the most ambitious law must be the one in Kirkland, Illinois, where bees are forbidden from flying over the town!

Source: Adapted from Nigel Blundell, The World's Greatest Mistakes (Hamlyn, 1991), p 35.

Bible references: Romans 3:19–21; 6:14–15; Galatians 3:10–13, 23–25; 4:4–5; 5:18; Colossians 2:20–23.

213. LIFE (Crime, Death, Doctors, Judgement, Medicine, Mistakes, Money, Sickness, Stealing, Humour)

Doctors told an American named Craig Boyden, who was just thirty-two, that he was suffering from Crohn's disease and had three months to live. Perhaps understandably, he decided that if he only had three months, he'd better make the most of them. He went back to his job as a credit manager at a carpet company in Elliott City in Maryland, and embezzled $30,000. He then used the money to live it up – dining in the best restaurants, throwing parties for his friends, buying drinks for everyone in every bar he went into.

But the funny thing was that as the weeks went by, instead of feeling worse and worse he just felt fine, if anything, even better than he had done. So he went to a different doctor for a second opinion. There he discovered that he wasn't suffering from Crohn's disease at all, but just a hernia. He'd suffered an allergic reaction to the gloves that the surgeon was wearing during exploratory surgery, and that had led to the misdiagnosis.

But that left him with another problem: the firm had found out that $30,000 was missing. Fortunately for Boyden, when he explained everything, the court was understanding, and gave him a suspended sentence, on condition that he paid the money back at the rate of $5,000 a year.

Source: Adapted from Bill Bryson, Bizarre World (Warner Books, 1995), pp 13–14.

Bible references: Psalms 39:4–6; 90:5–10; 103:15–16; Ecclesiastes 9:4–10; Isaiah 22:13; Matthew 24:45–51; Luke 12:42–46; 1 Corinthians 4:1–5; 7:29–31; 2 Peter 3:8–9.

214. MODERN LIFE (Belief, Cathedrals, Church, the Creed, Denominations, Holy Communion, Homosexuality, Hymns, Liberalism, Liturgy, Morality, New Age, Sex, Spirituality)

Traditional Christian believers visiting the Cathedral of Hope in Dallas, Texas, are in for a shock. It's not like any other cathedral they've been to before. It is the flagship of an openly homosexual denomination, founded in California in the 1960s, the Universal Fellowship of Metropolitan Community Churches. The church has very untraditional ideas about what constitutes sin, especially when it comes to matters of sex. Its leaders believe that your love life is your own business. If you want multiple partners, that's fine, as long as no one gets hurt. If you're into group sex, that's OK, too, as long as it's safe. And if you've got a thing about leather, you'll find there's a special prayer group you can join.

The liturgy is different, too. Hymns with supposedly sexist language such as 'Dear Lord and Father of Mankind' or 'Faith of our Fathers' are out, judged 'no more appropriate than the racist chants of the Ku Klux Klan'. The creed begins, 'We believe in God the Creator of us all whose desire for diversity is seen in the rainbow of humanity.' There's no mention of the virgin birth or the resurrection, although Jesus is included, as 'the Christ who is the embodiment of God's redeeming grace'. And teenagers are encouraged to celebrate communion with Diet Coke and nacho chips. It's very much a church of our time, where people construct their own beliefs and their own ceremonies.

And that attracts not only lesbian and gay people to the church, but heterosexual worshippers, too, in small but increasing numbers. In the significant words of the journalist who visited the church, they 'feel that this is the most alluring product in the spiritual supermarket'.

Source: Adapted from The Telegraph magazine, February 1999.

Bible references: Romans 1:24,26–28; 12:1–2; 1 Corinthians 6:9–20; Ephesians 4:17–24; 5:3–12; 1 Thessalonians 4:3–8; 2 Timothy 3:1–5; 4:3.

215. NATURE (Animals, Creation, Hardship, Hiking, Holidays, Human nature, Insects, Intolerance, Modern life, Mountains, Walking, Wilderness, Wildlife, Humour)

In an increasingly urbanised culture, it seems as if American tourists are finding the realities of being out in the countryside a little too – well, natural. On cards provided by the American Forest Service in wilderness areas visitors wrote the following comments:

- 'Too many bugs and leeches and spiders and spider webs. Please spray the wilderness to rid the area of these pests.'
- 'There are too many rocks in the mountains.'
- 'The coyotes made too much noise last night and kept me awake. Please eradicate these annoying animals.'
- 'Trails need to be wider so people can walk holding hands.'
- 'A small deer came into my camp and stole my bag of pickles. Is there a way I can get reimbursed?'
- 'Escalators would help on steep uphill sections.'
- 'A McDonald's would help at the trailhead.'

Source: Quoted in The Sunday Times, 16 August 1998.

216. SABBATH (Bible, Creation, History, Kissing, Law, Old Testament, Pharisees, Puritans, Shaving)

The early American Code of Connecticut included the following laws:

> No one shall run on the Sabbath Day, or walk in his garden, or elsewhere except reverently to and from meeting. No one shall travel, cook victuals, make beds, sweep house, cut hair, or shave on the Sabbath. If any man shall kiss his wife, or wife her husband on the Lord's Day, the party in fault shall be punished at the discretion of the court of magistrates.

Source: Quoted in Philip Yancey, What's So Amazing about Grace? (Zondervan, 1997), p 235.

Bible references: Exodus 20:8–11; 23:12; 31:12–17; 34:21; Deuteronomy 5:12–15; Nehemiah 13:15–22; Jeremiah 17:19–22; Matthew 12:1–14; 23:23–24; Mark 2:23–28; 3:1–6; Luke 6:1–11; 11:42; 13:10–16; 14:1–6; John 5:1–18; 7:22–24; 9:13–16; Romans 3:19–21; Galatians 4:9–10; 5:18; Colossians 2:16–17,20–23.

217. SCIENCE (Belief, Faith, Intercession, Prayer, God)

Is there a conflict between science and faith? A survey carried out among scientists in the United States in 1997 discovered that no fewer than 40% of biologists, physicists and mathematicians believed in a God who intervenes in human life. That is to say, according to the survey's strict definition, a God who 'actively communicates with the human race', and to whom we can pray 'in expectation of receiving an answer'. Despite the decline of faith in the West in the twentieth century, this figure of 40% matches the result of a similar survey carried out in 1916. Clearly for these scientists, there is no conflict between their scientific principles and their personal faith. As the novelist Fay Weldon has pointed out, 'God has become, oddly, something which almost only scientists believe in.'

Source: Adapted from The Church of England Newspaper, 25 April 1997; The Daily Telegraph, 14 June 1997.

Bible references: Psalm 8:3–4; Acts 17:22–28; Romans 1:20.

218. TITLES (Academics, Animals, Clergy, Dogs, Ordination, Qualifications, Scholarship, Humour)

In California, an individual named Venture has been awarded twelve university degrees and ordained as a minister. What makes this remarkable is that Venture is a labrador. His owner, Dr Diana Dawne, applied for the qualifications to show how easy it is to get awards by mail order in the United States. Venture's degree subjects included psychology, philosophy, law, archaeology and, naturally, zoology.

Source: Adapted from The Week, 1 March 1997.

Bible references: 1 Timothy 3:1–13; Titus 1:6–9.

219. UNBELIEF (Afterlife, Ascension, Belief, Bible, Bishops, Christ, Christianity, Creation, the Cross, God, History, Homosexuality, Incarnation, Intercession, Liberalism, Miracles, Morality, Myth, Prayer, Resurrection, Secularism, Theology, Virgin birth)

In 1998 the American bishop John Spong published a list of twelve Theses on the Internet, calling for a radical reformation which wouldn't just affect the church, but the whole nature of Christian belief. They were:

1. Theism, as a way of defining God, is dead. So most theological God-talk is today meaningless. A new way to speak of God must be found.
2. Since God can no longer be conceived in theistic terms, it becomes nonsensical to seek to understand Jesus as the incarnation of the theistic deity. So the Christology of the ages is bankrupt.
3. The biblical story of the perfect and finished creation from which human beings fell into sin is pre-Darwinian mythology and post-Darwinian nonsense.
4. The virgin birth, understood as literal biology, makes Christ's divinity, as traditionally understood, impossible.
5. The miracle stories of the New Testament can no longer be interpreted in a post-Newtonian world as supernatural events performed by an incarnate deity.
6. The view of the cross as the sacrifice for the sins of the world is a barbarian idea based on primitive concepts of God and must be dismissed.
7. Resurrection is an action of God. Jesus was raised into the meaning of God. It therefore cannot be a

physical resuscitation occurring inside human history.

8. The story of the ascension assumed a three-tier universe and is therefore not capable of being translated into the concepts of a post-Copernican age.
9. There is no external, objective, revealed standard writ in Scripture or on tablets of stone that will govern our ethical behaviour for all time.
10. Prayer cannot be a request made to a theistic deity to act in human history in a particular way.
11. The hope for life after death must be separated for ever from the behaviour control mentality of reward and punishment. The church must abandon, therefore, its reliance on guilt as a motivator of behaviour.
12. All human beings bear God's image and must be respected for what each person is. Therefore, no external description of one's being, whether based on race, ethnicity, gender or sexual orientation, can properly be used as the basis for either rejection or discrimination.

Source: Quoted in The Church of England Newspaper, 15 May 1998.

Bible references: Genesis 1 – 3; Matthew 1:18–25; 6:9–10; 16:27; 25:14–46; 28:1–10; Mark 16:1–8; Luke 1:30–35; 6:23; 11:1–2; 18:1–7; 24:1–43,50–51; John 5:28–29; 10:37–38; 14:11; 20:1–8,17; Acts 1:1–9; 2:22; Romans 3:23; 16:17–18; 1 Corinthians 3:10–15; 15:1–8; Galatians 1:6–9; Ephesians 5:2; 6:7–8; Colossians 3:23–25; 1 Timothy 2:1–4; 2 Timothy 4:3; Hebrews 1:3; 9:26; 10:10–14; James 5:16–18; 2 Peter 2:1–2; 1 John 2:2; 4:10.

220. UNLIKELY MESSIAHS – Elvis Presley (Belief, Christ, End times, False prophets, Gullibility, Judgement, Myth, New Age, New Testament, Prediction, Prophecy, Resurrection, Visions, Voice of God)

American Robert Campbell said:

> I found myself in Paradise, and very suddenly I saw this all but blinding white light, and then a voice that sounded very similar to a roll of thunder, and yet it was very recognisable: the words were clear as day. And I was told by the voice coming out of the light: 'Go back and tell them – Elvis.'
>
> He's Immanuel, the only-begotten son God promised he would send. Not only would he send him to the tribes of Israel, but he would send him to the Gentiles also. Immanuel and Elvis are synonymous. He's the Son of God – no question about it. The very incarnation of [sic]. I'm convinced he was also led to the slaughter like the lamb.
>
> [The story of Jesus in the Gospels] is not only a legend and a myth, but it's based on a prophecy that was going to come true.
>
> The risen Elvis has been seen. He will come and judge the earth with his what is known as the feather of truth. And that will be Judgement Day. Relatively speaking, that's very soon. It's got to be within ten years, and most likely closer to five years, maybe even less.

Source: Elvis and the Presleytarians: Worshipping the King, BBC TV, 17 August 1997.

Bible references: Isaiah 53:7; Matthew 24:4–5,11,23–27; Mark 13:5–6,21–22; Luke 17:23; 21:8; Acts 8:32–35; 2 Peter 2:1–2; 1 John 4:1.

CAN YOU BELIEVE IT?

221. AMAZING DISCOVERIES (Bible, Books, the Cross, Jesus, New Testament, Relics, Humour)

If you want to write a best-seller about Jesus, it's no good repeating the story that's in the Bible. And if you want to make a lot of money from your book, you need to come up with a really unusual new twist to the story. Just look at the range of books which claim to have discovered the last resting place of the remains of Jesus. In *The Tomb of God,* published in 1996, two self-styled experts, a diver and an engineer, claimed that they had broken secret codes in documents, paintings and monuments to locate the burial place of Jesus near Rennes-le-Château in southern France. As in so many books of this kind, it was said to be the Knights Templar who had preserved the secret over the centuries.

The Templars crop up again in another book, written two years later, *The Head of God: the Lost Treasure of the Templars*. This author claimed that the head of Jesus is not in Languedoc, but embalmed in a secret vault in a small chapel outside Rosslyn Castle in the west of Scotland. He admitted that he hadn't been able to open the vault to make sure, but said that his research had proved that it was there.

The three authors of yet another book, *The Holy Kingdom*, published in 1998, were sure that they had found another important Christian relic in Britain, namely the cross on which Jesus was crucified – in South Wales. Sadly, they, too, were unable to prove their case by opening the cave where the cross was supposed to be hidden, just outside the village of Nevern near Fishguard, and marked by a cross carved in the cliff. But they did say that a friend of theirs had actually seen the cross by moving some of the stones at the mouth of the cave.

Source: Adapted from Richard Andrews and Paul Schellenberger, The Tomb of God (Little, Brown and Company, 1996); The Daily Telegraph, 21 November 1998.

Bible references: Matthew 27:31–35; Mark 15:20–24; Luke 23:33; John 19:16–18.

222. BIBLE STUDY (Death, Eccentrics, Healing, Sickness, Humour)

The Emperor Menelik II of Ethiopia took the injunction to 'Read, mark, learn and inwardly digest' the Scriptures a bit too literally. Whenever he was ill he used to eat a few pages of the Bible in the belief that it would cure him. This went on for some years until he suffered a stroke in December 1913, and attempted to eat the entire book of Kings. He died before he managed to finish it.

Source: Adapted from Peter Gammons, All Preachers Great and Small (Minstrel, 1989), p 59; Geoffrey Regan, Histrionics (Robson Books, 1994), p 102.

Bible references: Deuteronomy 8:3; Job 23:12; Psalms 19:9–10; 119:103; Matthew 4:4; Luke 4:4; 2 Timothy 3:14–17.

223. BOOKS (Eccentrics, End times, False prophets, God, Mathematics, Rapture, Second Coming, Shouting, Theology, Humour)

Who today remembers

- *Mathematical Principles of Theology, or the Existence of God Geometrically Demonstrated* by Richard Jack?

Or George Henry's unforgettable trilogy

- *Demonstration of the Spirit Originally Called Shouting*, published by the Holiness Movement Publishing House in 1908, and
- *History of the Jumpers*, published by the Metropolitan Church Association the following year. These followed his first, self-published work
- *Shouting, Genuine and Spurious*, which came out half a century earlier.

Finally, how many booksellers still have remaindered copies of Edgar Whisenant's book

- *88 Reasons Why the Rapture Will be in 1988*? 4.5 million of them were published, and they sold like hot cakes – until the end of 1988. Undaunted, Whisenant revised the book and republished it the following year with the title:
- *The Final Shout – Rapture Report 1989*!

Source: Quoted in Russell Ash and Brian Lake, Bizarre Books (Macmillan, 1985), p 142; Russell Chandler, Doomsday (Word, 1993), p 273.

Bible references: Ecclesiastes 12:12; Matthew 24:36–42; 25:13; Mark 13:32–37; Acts 1:7.

224. EYE-WITNESS (Archaeology, Clergy, Death, Eccentrics, Evidence, Proof, Relics, Remembering, Resurrection, Testimony, Humour)

Three years after Oliver Cromwell's death, an angry mob of royalists dug up his body, chopped off the head and impaled it on top of a wall in Westminster. For most of the next 300 years, the head disappeared, and nobody knew where it was.

On an autumn day in 1956 a couple were out painting in Suffolk. Suddenly there was a torrential downpour, and they took shelter under a nearby oak tree, which was a few yards away from a house. After a few minutes the door of the house opened and a maid came out holding an umbrella. She invited them to come in out of the rain, and offered them a cup of coffee.

An old gentleman was waiting in the hall. He introduced himself as Canon Wilkinson, and he was obviously pleased to have some company. Soon the three of them were sitting by the fire, deep in conversation, when the old clergyman said he had something to show them, something they wouldn't forget. He brought back an oblong black box, and took off the lid. Inside, wrapped in dark red silk, was the head of Oliver Cromwell, still impaled on a pike. The eyes were sunken and the nose had started to fall apart, but the head still had plenty of hair and they could clearly see the famous wart.

For those who like to know such things, Canon Wilkinson died not long afterwards, and the head was finally reburied in 1960, in Sidney Sussex College in Cambridge. But the old man was right: that couple never did forget what they had seen in that black box that autumn day in Suffolk.

Source: Adapted from CAM, Michaelmas 1996 and Easter 1997.

Bible references: Luke 1:1–2; John 1:14; 2 Peter 1:16–18; 1 John 1:1–3.

225. THE MEANING OF LIFE (Experience, Philosophy, Humour)

In his book, *A History of Western Philosophy,* Bertrand Russell quoted the case of a man who was sure that he had discovered the secret of the universe, but was only aware of it when he was under the influence of laughing-gas. The trouble was that as soon as the effects of the gas wore off, the man forgot what the secret was. After a whole series of attempts, he finally managed to write it down before he forgot it. When he had completely recovered he rushed over to see what he had written. It was, 'A smell of petroleum prevails throughout.'

Source: Adapted from Bill Bryson, Neither Here nor There (Minerva, 1992), frontispiece.

Bible references: Job 11:7–9; Ecclesiastes 3:11; 8:17; Isaiah 40:28; Romans 11:33–34.

226. NAMES (Baptism, Children, Clergy, Eccentrics, Families, Fathers, Humour)

In a letter to *The Times,* Robert Maxtone Graham wrote about the bizarre series of names which a relative of his, who was rector of South Witham in Lincolnshire in the late nineteenth century, gave his fourteen children. There was a family tradition of using the name Lyonel, with a y, so that was the name given to the eldest son. Variations on the theme then followed, with the boys being given names like Leo, Leone, and Lyonulph, and the girls being given names such as Lyonesse, Lyona, Lyonella and Lyonetta. One poor boy ended up with sixteen Christian names: Lyulph Ydwallo Odin Nestor Egbert Lyonel Toedmag Hugh Erchenwyne Saxon Esa Cromwell Orma Nevill Dysart Plantagenet Tollemache-

Tollemache. The idea was that the initials spelled out Lyonel the Second. He emigrated to New Zealand: who can blame him?

Source: Adapted from The Times, 20 July 1999.

227. NEW AGE (Alternative medicine, Belief, Disability, Faith healing, Forgiveness, Healing, Punishment, Reincarnation, Retribution, Sickness, Sin, Suffering)

Eileen Drewery hit the headlines in the 1990s when Glenn Hoddle, the England football coach, said how much she'd helped him as a faith healer. Hoddle was forced to resign when he repeated her idea that disabled people may be paying for the sins of a past life. It's hard to see how he could claim that he'd been misunderstood, because Mrs Drewery was very open about what she believed. For instance, her ten-year-old grandson had asthma, and she wasn't able to cure him. 'What did my grandson do in a previous life?' she wondered. 'It might be that he caused a lot of problems with our fellow man, say in breathing... perhaps he let off a gas bomb or something.' Or then there was her husband, who had to wear a colostomy bag. She and he were sitting watching the film 'Braveheart' together, when a character was disembowelled. 'I sort of said to Eileen, perhaps that's what I was up to in the last time round,' said Mr Drewery. 'A bit flippant really.' But she took it seriously, and ended up persuading her husband that he may have been an executioner in a previous life. As G.K. Chesterton said, when people stop believing in God, they don't believe in nothing, they believe in anything.

Source: Adapted from The Daily Telegraph, 20 March 1999.

Bible references: Deuteronomy 13:1–3; Matthew 7:21–23; 2 Timothy 4:3–4; 1 John 4:1–3.

228. SAINTS (History, Miracles, Protection, Relics, Travel)

In days gone by long-distance travel was fraught with danger, and in the sixth and seventh centuries Christians often carried amulets for spiritual protection, which were called *eulogia*. The most precious were those containing holy relics. They wouldn't be actual bones, since ordinary people couldn't afford those, but dust from places where the saints had been. One miracle text tells how a monk was on a sea voyage when a storm blew up. The captain was all prepared to abandon ship, but fortunately the monk was carrying a little container of earth from the base of the column of Simeon Stylites, the sixth-century saint who lived on top of a pillar. Then 'the monk took the dust of the saintly servant of God that he carried with him as a blessing, and after having put it into water, he threw it on the sea and sprinkled all the boat, saying, "Holy servant of God, Simeon, direct us and save us." With these words, all those on the boat were impregnated with perfume, the sea water surrounded the boat like a wall, and the waves were powerless against it.'

Simeon's dust was also famous for its healing powers. Other stories told how it cured a sick donkey, caused hair to grow on a bald man's head, and made a vat of sour wine sweet again.

Source: Adapted from Biblical Archaeology Review, July – August 1997.

Bible references: Exodus 15:23–25; 2 Kings 2:19–22; 4:38–41; Psalm 107:23–28; Jonah 1:4–15; Matthew 8:23–27; Mark 4:35–41; Luke 8:22–25; Acts 19:11–12.

229. SAINTS (Amazing discoveries, Church, Miracles, Relics, Humour)

When the chapel where St Beuno was said to be buried was being renovated, they had to open the tomb which was supposed to contain the saint's body. The archaeologists who examined the bones were astonished to discover that nestling within the body's pelvis was the skeleton of a foetus. They quietly reported the find to the church authorities, thinking that this would be a cause of great embarrassment. But they weren't in the least put out. 'St Beuno,' they commented, 'was a very remarkable man.'

Source: Adapted from Geoffrey Regan, Histrionics (Robson Books, 1994), p 73.

230. SIGNS (Belief, Evidence, Faith, God, Jesus, Mary, Miracles, Proof, Humour)

In 1997 a window cleaner in Weston-super-Mare was sitting watching television and eating a packet of crisps when suddenly he saw a vision of Jesus and the Virgin Mary on one of the crisps. 'You can see Mary's nose, mouth and shawl,' he said. 'Her head is slightly bowed as she cradles the baby Jesus. I knew I had stumbled upon something special. It's not every day you come across a religious crisp.' The man, whose name is Alan Puddy, said that he knew some people would laugh at him. 'These things come to us as a sign,' he said. 'I've been given an opportunity to find my true path in life. I was never much of a churchgoer, but this has proved to me that there is a God.'

Source: Adapted from The Daily Telegraph, 6 September 1997.

Bible references: John 1:14; Acts 9:3–6; 18:9–10; 22:6–9,17–18; 26:13–15; 1 Corinthians 9:1; 15:3–8; 2 Corinthians 12:1–4; 2 Peter 1:16–18; 1 John 1:1–3.

231. SIGNS (Belief, Business, Faith, Giving, Mary, Miracles, Money, Humour)

On 17 December 1996 a customer on her way to the offices of the Seminole Finance Company in Florida was struck by the shape of some large coloured stains on the windows of the building. The more she looked, the clearer the image seemed: it was the Virgin Mary, about thirty-five feet high, her hood and shoulders in yellow and blue, her tunic a swirling mixture of purple, green and orange, her face a gentle pink. She rang a local TV station, they broadcast pictures that afternoon, and by nightfall there were 700 people in the parking lot, with flowers, candles, and prayer requests on bits of paper.

Over the next three months it is reckoned that over half a million people came to see the figure. They prayed, took pictures, lit candles, or just looked. Some gave money: during the first three months more than $40,000 was collected for local charities. Other people brought their own miracles: one man was showing passers-by an old frying pan covered in rust, which he thought formed the outline of a sheep. 'You see?' he said, 'It's the lamb of Christ.'

Source: Adapted from The Telegraph magazine, 3 March 1997.

Bible references: John 1:14; Acts 9:3–6; 18:9–10; 22:6–9,17–18; 26:13–15; 1 Corinthians 9:1; 15:3–8; 2 Corinthians 12:1–4; 2 Peter 1:16–18; 1 John 1:1–3.

232. SUFFERING (Answered prayer, Church, God, Hardship, Healing, Law courts, Music, Old age, Sickness, Humour)

In March 1999 the *Church of England Newspaper* reported a law suit brought by a sixty-three-year-old man in New York against God. The man, whose name was Donald Drusky, argued that 'Defendant God is the sovereign ruler of the universe and took no corrective action against the leaders of his church and his nation for their extremely serious wrongs, which ruined the life of Donald S. Drusky.' More specifically, Mr Drusky claimed that God should have given him the same musical skills as his favourite guitarists, and shouldn't have robbed him of his youth. The court dismissed his case.

Such things could only happen in America, you may think. Not so! In 1981 a Ghanaian spiritual leader filed a lawsuit at the High Court in Accra against God, Jesus Christ, and four local church leaders, claiming damages from all of them for 'unlawfully afflicting him with plague and calamity' over the previous eight years and seven months. Unfortunately on that occasion the outcome of the trial was not reported.

Source: Adapted from The Church of England Newspaper, 26 March 1999; Punch, September 1981.

Bible references: Job 9 – 10; 13; 23; 30:20–31; Psalms 10; 13:1–4; 44:9–25; 88.

233. UNLIKELY MESSIAHS (Bible, Christ, Cults, Death, False prophets, God, Immortality, Jesus, Morality, New religious movements, Prediction, Prophecy, Sects, Smoking)

In 1950 a fisherman from North Holland named Louwrens van Voorthuizen declared that he was God. Lou, as he preferred to be called, gathered a small but very committed group of followers around him, saying that his role was similar to that of Jesus, but greater, because Jesus had only won a spiritual victory over the devil, whereas he, Lou, would defeat the devil in the body and become immortal.

He rejected traditional Christian morality as outdated and irrelevant. 'Why shouldn't God smoke?' he would ask, puffing away on his cigar. Now that God was once again here on earth in human form – in him – the Bible was superseded. So in the tracts which his followers gave out on the streets of Amsterdam, Lou mocked the Bible and the clergy who preached it. He predicted that the end of time was near, when his followers – most of whom were middle-aged and female – would all become immortal, too. His claims rather lost their credibility when Lou died in 1968, and the group died out not long afterwards.

Source: Adapted from Encyclopedia of World Religions (Octopus Books, 1975), pp 237–238.

Bible references: Matthew 7:15–23; 24:4–5,11,23–24; Mark 13:5–6, 21–22; Luke 17:23; 21:8; 2 Thessalonians 2:4; 2 Peter 2:1–3; 1 John 4:1.

234. 666 (The Beast, Cars, Demons, Exorcism, New Age, Paganism, Revelation, Witchcraft, Humour)

Kevin Carlyon, who calls himself the High Priest of the covenant of Earth Magic, is often in the papers, undoubtedly because some of his exploits are so bizarre. In 1997, for instance, he exorcised a Ford Capri in Eastbourne because it had the registration number ARK 666Y. As Kevin explained to the *Eastbourne Gazette*, 'The mark of the beast is 666, and without our expert help, there could have been a few problems. It is a nasty, evil little piece of work, but we feel we have made it safe now.' The owner wasn't so worried about the car being demonic; he said, 'I am not really convinced by it at all, but the car's going in for its MOT soon, so we shall see.'

Kevin and Sandra, his 'high priestess', also tried to use magic to stop developers building fifty-three houses on a piece of land at Beltinge. He said he was going to leave a talisman at the site which would draw upon the powers of nature to protect the local wildlife, deter the developers, and even influence the planning committee in Canterbury. 'We are 100% serious in what we do,' said Mr Carlyon. 'There are no devils or demons involved. We are normal people.'

Source: Adapted from The Daily Telegraph, 15 February 1997.

Bible references: Revelation 13:11–18.

HOW NOT TO...

235. CHURCH (Baptism, Boredom, Children, Clergy, Damnation, How others see us, Hymns, Judgement, Modern life, Music, Preaching, Relevance, Sermons, Sin, Songs, the Trinity, Witness)

When Boy George visited a church for a baptism, he was profoundly unimpressed. This is what he wrote in the *Daily Mail* afterwards:

> Churches are glorious places, but don't you wish they were a little more inviting? On Sunday I attended the christening of my year-old godson Michael and he was as restless as everyone else.
>
> The grown-ups were content to squirm inwardly and eye their watches. Michael was much more honest and aired his discomfort with a holler.
>
> The sermon was based on The Holy Trinity as it was Trinity Sunday, but because I never go to church it was like explaining Shakespeare to a groundhog.
>
> The priest was a lovely man with impeccable dress sense but I was confused from the moment he took to the pulpit. Most of us only ever go to church for weddings and funerals, so sticking to the book is pointless.

Only a religious trainspotter would know the stories by heart and what is the point of rattling on about sin when most of us are doomed to eternal damnation? It doesn't warm people to Christianity, it only makes them feel like hypocrites.

Worse still are the utterly depressing hymns. I'd like to see live music, acoustic guitars and percussion. An old Fairy liquid bottle filled with dried peas would do just fine.

Church should be a joyous and liberating experience. Little Michael should have been carried in on a fresh-fruit platter and we should have sung, 'He's Got the Whole World in His Hands' or 'Michael, Row the Boat Ashore'.

The church badly needs a facelift because it is God's theatre on earth and he should be packing them in. Amen.

Source: The 'Outside Edge' column in The Daily Mail, copyright © 1998 The Daily Mail. Reproduced with kind permission.

Bible references: 1 Corinthians 10:32–33.

236. EVANGELISM (Boldness, Courage, Communication, Death, Fear, the Gospel, Trains, Witness, Humour)

The evangelist Justyn Rees tells the story of his great uncle Willie. He was a tall, gaunt man, who used to wear a black suit and a black overcoat which made him look like an undertaker. That impression was reinforced by his face, with its hollow, sunken cheeks and his strong, determined jaw. Behind it all he was really a shy man, who preferred to keep himself to himself. But at the same time, he believed that he should try to share the gospel with everyone he met, wherever he was.

One day he was sitting on a train in an otherwise empty compartment, and so he prayed that the Lord would send a fellow passenger that he could share his faith with. At the next station a teenage girl got on board, who glanced nervously at Willie sitting in the seat opposite. The train started, and Willie tried to pluck up the courage to say something. It took him a few minutes, as he was trying to work out what to say. All this time his steady stare made the girl sitting opposite feel more and more uncomfortable, but she couldn't go anywhere, because it was one of those old carriages which didn't have any connecting doors.

Eventually Willie plucked up the courage to speak. It happened to be just as the train was going into a tunnel, but he hadn't noticed that. He cleared his throat, leant forward and said in his deep, resonant voice, 'Are you ready to die?' At the same moment, everything went dark. The girl screamed, pulled the communication cord, and the train screeched to a halt. Justyn Rees doesn't actually say so, but presumably the girl wasn't converted on the spot.

Source: Adapted from Justyn Rees, Love Your Neighbour for God's Sake, reproduced in Renewal, March 1998.

Bible references: Matthew 10:16; 28:18–20; Luke 9:60; Romans 10:14–15; 1 Corinthians 10:32–33; Colossians 4:5–6; 2 Timothy 4:2; 1 Peter 3:15–16.

237. EVANGELISM (Arguments, Christian Science, Confidence, Cults, the Gospel, Jehovah's Witnesses, Love, Salvation, Sects, Witness)

In the book, *Why We Left a Cult,* six different men and women from the United States talk about their involvement in either the Jehovah's Witnesses, Christian

Science, or the New Age movement. Although their experiences are naturally very different, on one point their stories are very similar.
Joan Cetnar, a former Jehovah's Witness, said

> To be honest, I cannot remember anyone who ever really tried to talk to me about Christ. There were people who said they were Christians and then slammed the door in my face, or who wanted to argue about why Witnesses wouldn't salute the flag. Considering all the doors I knocked on, I recall plenty of arguments about the Trinity and other doctrines, but no one ever talked to me about being born again or about accepting Jesus as my personal Saviour and having that assurance of salvation.

Carolyn Poole was a Christian Scientist, but she found the same:

> Even at points where I was disillusioned with Christian Science and was attending other churches, no one ever talkd to me directly about how Jesus was not correctly taught in Christian Science. I have counselled many people who have left the Christian Science church, and most of us have had similar experiences. Christians would tell you about how refusing to go to a doctor was wrong, but they never took the time to sit down with you and show you in the Gospels who Jesus is.

Source: Quoted in Latayne C. Scott, ed., Why We Left a Cult (Baker Books, 1993), pp 102–103.

Bible references: Matthew 10:16; 28:18–20; Romans 10:14–15; 1 Corinthians 10:32–33; Colossians 4:5–6; 2 Timothy 4:2; James 5:19–20; 1 Peter 3:15–16; Jude 22–23.

238. HEALING (Failure, Ministry, Prayer, Sickness, Humour)

Bryn Jones has undoubtedly been one of the most important figures in the house church movement in Britain. But his first steps in the healing ministry were pretty disastrous. He was in Norfolk in an evangelistic team with two other men, Derek and Bob, and they advertised publicly that they were going to hold some Christian healing meetings. Next morning, Bryn woke up covered in a rash. In his own words, 'I tried everything to get rid of it, including looking at myself in a mirror and rebuking what I could see, but to no avail.'

Next morning it was Derek's turn. He woke up to find his neck so stiff he could hardly move it. They called in a nurse, who said it would clear up in a few days. To make matters worse, that afternoon Bob was stung by a wasp. Within hours his arm had swollen up so much he needed a sling. Bryn goes on, 'So the three of us went to the meeting that evening, me covered in a rash, Derek with his head stuck, and Bob in a sling... We decided to postpone the meeting.'

Within a few days they were all recovered enough to have another go. They decided to pray for a disabled lady who lived in a house beside the church. Bryn describes the scene:

> When we arrived we stood around the woman, who had a little kitten on her lap, and began praying. I said, 'I know what this is. It's a spirit of infirmity.' So I said to the spirit, 'In the name of Jesus Christ, come out of her.' With that the kitten did three leaps in the air – and dropped dead. I think I must be the only preacher who, on his first divine healing crusade, succeeded in killing the cat! I might add that the woman didn't seem to improve either.

Source: Adapted from Brian Hewitt, Doing a New Thing? (Hodder and Stoughton, 1995), pp 12–13.

Bible references: Matthew 10:1,8; Mark 6:5,12–13; Luke 9:2; 10:9; Acts 5:12–16; 28:8–9; 2 Corinthians 12:7–10; Philippians 2:25–30; James 5:14–16.

239. LEADERSHIP (Communication, Foot in mouth, Honesty, Misunderstanding, Politics, Promises, Vision, War, Humour)

Good leaders have to have a vision. And effective leaders have to be able to communicate that vision. Theodore Roosevelt became famous in America as a result of his leadership at the battle of San Juan in the Cuban war. When he campaigned to become governor of New York in 1898, some of the 'Rough riders' who had fought under him went to speak in his support. Unfortunately they hadn't been rehearsed in what to say. At one stop ex-Sergeant Buck said to the crowd. 'I want to talk to you about my colonel. He kept every promise he made to us and he will to you. When he took us to Cuba he told us we would have to lie out in the trenches with the rifle bullets climbing all over us, and we done it... He told us we might meet wounds and death and we done it... And when it came to the great day he led us up San Juan hill like sheep to the slaughter, and so he will lead you.'

Source: Adapted from Geoffrey Regan, Histrionics (Robson Books, 1994), p 166.

Bible references: Ezekiel 34:2–6; 1 Thessalonians 5:12–13; 1 Timothy 3:1–13; Titus 1:6–9; Hebrews 13:7,17; 1 Peter 5:2–3.

240. PERSEVERANCE (Conversion, Discipleship, Endurance, Hardship, Prison, Suffering, Humour)

Jerry Wolfson managed to escape from Norwich prison. However, just two hours later he knocked on the gate and asked to be let back in. He said that he was cold and wet, and he had torn his trousers in an embarrassing place.

Source: Adapted from Bill Bryson, Bizarre World (Warner Books, 1995), p 41.

Bible references: Isaiah 40:30–31; Luke 8:15; Romans 2:7–8; 5:3–4; 1 Corinthians 9:24–27; 2 Corinthians 6:4–10; Galatians 6:9; Colossians 1:10–11; 1 Thessalonians 1:3; 2 Thessalonians 1:4; 3:13; 1 Timothy 4:16; 2 Timothy 2:3–6,10–13; 4:5; Hebrews 12:1–3; James 1:2–4,12; 5:11.

241. PERSEVERANCE (Air travel, Boredom, Flying, Frustration, Stupidity, Vision, Humour)

Larry Walters wanted to be a pilot, but the US Air Force turned him down, and he got bored and frustrated being a truck driver. So one day he hit on a novel way of making himself airborne. He went to his local army surplus store and bought up their entire stock of weather balloons. That day they happened to have forty-five. He filled them with helium and tied them to a chair which he had anchored to the bumper of his jeep. He armed himself with an air rifle, so that he could burst a few balloons when he wanted to come down again, sat in the chair, and cut himself loose.

To his surprise, instead of floating gently upwards, the chair shot up into the air as if it was jet propelled, and soon Mr Walters found himself floating at 11,000 feet. He was up there for a full fourteen hours before he drifted into the approach to Los Angeles international airport. A rather bemused Pan Am pilot radioed that he had just passed a man in a chair, armed with a gun, at 11,000 feet. The reaction of air traffic control is unfortunately not recorded.

Fortunately for Larry Walters, who was by now heading out to sea, the pilot's report was taken seriously. A Navy helicopter was scrambled, the crew lowered a rope and towed him back to safety. As the LA police were leading him away, someone asked Mr Walters why he'd done it. 'A man can't just sit around,' was his answer.

Source: Adapted from The Times, 24 April 1997.

242. PLANNING (Death, Experience, History, Possessions, Preparedness, Priorities, Wealth)

In 1845 the naval explorer John Franklin led a party of 138 officers and men to try to discover the Northwest passage between the Atlantic and the Pacific. With them they carried, among other things, a library of 1,200 books, a hand organ which could play fifty different tunes, china place settings for officers and men, cut glass wine goblets, and sterling silver tableware. The clothing they wore was the uniform of the Royal Navy, with no concessions made for the Arctic cold.

They all died, frozen in the ice. Their corpses were found alongside broken backgammon boards and silver table ornaments engraved with the officers' initials and their family crests.

Source: Adapted from Eugene Peterson, The Contemplative Pastor (Eerdmans, 1993), p 82.

Bible references: Proverbs 15:22; 16:9; 19:21; Matthew 6:19–21; 19:21–29; Mark 10:21–30; Luke 12:16–21,33–34; 14:28–33; 18:22–30; 1 Timothy 6:17–19; James 4:13–16.

243. PRAYER (Football, Opportunity, Preparedness, Priorities, Sport, Humour)

'Pray in the Spirit on all occasions,' says Paul, and 'pray continually,' but there are times when it's best not to get down on your knees, put your hands together and close your eyes. That was certainly what Brazilian goalkeeper Isadore Irandir discovered when his team Rio Preto was playing against Corinthians in the 1970s. He was still finishing his pre-match prayers when the referee blew the whistle to start the match. It wouldn't have mattered against most teams, but one of the Corinthians' strikers was the brilliant Roberto Rivelino. From the kick-off the ball was played to him, and when he noticed that the goalie was still on his knees, he picked his spot and shot from the half-way line. The ball hit the back of the net, and Corinthians had scored just three seconds after the kick-off!

Source: Adapted from Stephen Pile, The Book of Heroic Failures (Futura, 1980), p 105.

Bible references: Luke 18:1–7; Acts 1:14; Ephesians 6:18; Philippians 4:6; Colossians 4:2; 1 Thessalonians 5:17.

244. PREPAREDNESS (Bible, the Devil, Planning, Priorities, Snakes, Spiritual warfare, Temptation, Humour)

The US Peace Corps train their workers to deal with any kind of eventuality they might meet in the field, and since they work in the jungles of South America, it's quite possible that they might encounter an anaconda, the largest snake in the world. A full-grown anaconda isn't just a snake, it's a telegraph pole with a temper. It takes ten men to carry one – if it's in a good mood. Here are the instructions in one of the Peace Corps's manuals, which were posted on the Internet.

1. If you are attacked by an anaconda, do not run. The snake is faster than you are, so don't even try to outrun it.
2. Lie flat on the ground. Put your arms tight against your sides, your legs tight against one another.
3. Tuck in your chin.
4. The snake will come and begin to nudge, and climb about your body.
5. Do not panic.
6. After the snake has examined you, it will begin to swallow you from the feet. Always from the feet. Permit the snake to swallow your feet and ankles. Do not panic.
7. The snake will now begin to suck your legs into its body. You must lie perfectly still. This will take a long time.
8. When the snake has reached your knees, slowly and with as little movement as possible reach down, take your knife and very gently slide it into the side of the snake's mouth, between the edge of its mouth and your leg. Then suddenly rip upwards, severing the snake through the top of the head.
9. Be sure you have your knife.
10. Be sure your knife is sharp.

Of course, if you get to number 9, or even number 10, and find that you've forgotten your knife, or that it's blunt, the rest doesn't really matter!

Source: Adapted from James Ryle, New Wine, August 1997.

Bible references: Matthew 4:1–11; Luke 4:1–13; 22:31–32; 1 Corinthians 10:13; Ephesians 6:17; Hebrews 4:12; James 4:7; 1 Peter 5:8–9; Revelation 12:9.

245. SIN (Failure, Missing the mark, Shooting, Humour)

One of the terms that the Bible uses for sin is, more literally, 'missing the mark'. We try to do what is right, but don't quite make it. The Duke of Sussex was a notoriously bad shot. After one day's shooting at Holkham Hall the owner, Sir Edward Coke, gave him his score card, which read as follows:

> Killed of game: 0
> Wounded in the legs: 1 foot-marker
> Wounded in the face: 1 groom
> Wounded on the head of a friend: 1 hat
> Ditto on the left rump: 1 horse.

Source: Adapted from Geoffrey Regan, Histrionics (Robson Books, 1994), p 164.

Bible references: Genesis 3:1–7; Psalm 14:1–3; Proverbs 20:9; Ecclesiastes 7:20; Romans 3:9,23; 7:14–25.

246. WINNING AND LOSING (Cars, Endurance, Heaven, Life, Perseverance, Prize, Rally driving, Sport, Victory)

In the World Rally Championships in 1998 the Spanish driver Carlos Sainz drove nearly 15,000 miles across five continents. He only needed to come fourth in the last rally of the season to win his third world title, and at Margam Park in South Wales the spectators gathered at the finishing post to cheer him home. The first three cars tore across the finishing line, and Sainz was right behind them, cruising home in fourth place. He was just 300 metres from the end, with the finishing post – and the world championship – in sight, when the unthinkable happened. The engine burst into flames and the car coasted to a halt. Sainz clambered out and burst into tears. His co-driver kicked the car and threw his helmet at it. 300 metres from glory, but it might just as well have been 300 miles.

Source: Adapted from The Times, 25 November 1998.

Bible references: Ecclesiastes 9:11; Acts 20:24; 1 Corinthians 9:24–27; Galatians 2:2; 5:7; Philippians 2:16; 3:12–14; 2 Timothy 2:5; 4:7–8; Hebrews 12:1–3; James 1:12.

247. WITNESS (Bible, Cars, Evangelism, Hymns, Law, Parking, Preaching, Traffic wardens, Humour)

A traffic warden in Germany has come up with a novel way of cutting the number of people who park illegally. Instead of simply giving them a parking ticket, Otto Jantzer preaches at them. One of his victims said, 'I came back from the shop and he was standing next to my car. He got out his Bible and started reciting Psalm 88 about the wrath of God. Then he made me kneel down and sing a hymn.'

You might think that this would make Mr Jantzer unpopular with his employers, but the fact is that his unorthodox methods have been remarkably effective. There has been a dramatic drop in illegal parking, because nobody caught by him wants to repeat the experience. As one former offender commented, 'I always park in the multi-storey now!'

Source: Adapted from Tear Times, Spring 1998.

Bible references: Psalm 88; Matthew 28:18–20; Luke 9:60; Romans 10:14–15; 1 Corinthians 10:32–33; Colossians 4:5–6; 2 Timothy 4:2; 1 Peter 3:15–16.

SUBJECT INDEX

BIBLE REFERENCE INDEX

1 Corinthians